P9-EJS-682

Auguste Piccard

Auguste Piccard

Captain of Space

Admiral of the Abyss

By ADELAIDE FIELD

1969   HOUGHTON MIFFLIN COMPANY   BOSTON

INTRODUCTION

IN THIS BOOK Adelaide Field is offering to the rising generation the portrait of a man who was always a friend of the young. His physics laboratory at the University of Brussels was a workshop for his students, and for the friends and classmates of his children as well. It was not unusual for him to invite an entire class for experimental demonstrations. These aroused a passionate interest in his young listeners.

Auguste Piccard was an extraordinary teacher. He had no patience with the accepted procedure of memorizing without understanding. He led his pupils to an intelligent understanding of problems and experiments. He also led them to discover simple solutions, initiating them into the highest discipline of science.

He was personally dedicated, body and soul, to this discipline. He possessed the kind of authority which arouses enthusiasm and spurs performance. May you who read this book find in him an example and an inspiration, along the ofttimes difficult path of learning!

Marianne Denis Piccard
(Madame Auguste Piccard)

January, 1969, Lausanne, Switzerland

(Translated from Madame Piccard's French version.)

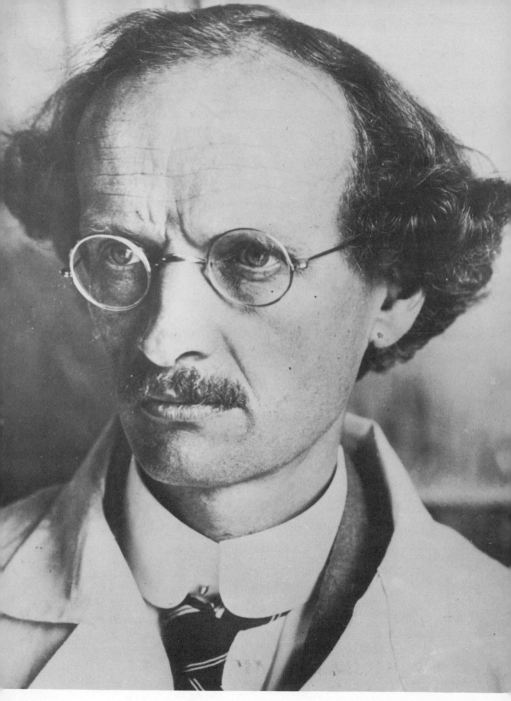

To discover new countries,
to climb the highest peaks,
to travel
through new areas of celestial space,
to turn our searchlights
upon domains of eternal darkness,
that is what makes life worth living.

AUGUSTE PICCARD* —

* Reprinted, by special permission of the publisher, from *Earth, Sky and Sea*, by Auguste Piccard, Oxford University Press, 1956.

Auguste Piccard

part 1

For untold centuries back into the corridors of time, earthbound man had dreamed of being able to fly. The caveman must have peered at the eagle's soaring flight and envied him his wings. Long before the birth of Christ, Greek mythologists wrote the imaginative story of Icarus who fashioned wings of wax and met disaster when he flew too close to the sun. Later, Leonardo da Vinci, Benjamin Franklin, Thomas Jefferson and many other multigifted men worked out elaborate drawings, even scale models, of "flying machines." Yet when man achieved his age-old dream and was able to fly high above the earth at will, he did not do it in a flying machine, *he did it in a balloon.*

Auguste Piccard, the hero of this book, flew higher in a balloon than any man had ever flown before him . . . into the upper regions of the stratosphere, where it had not been possible to sustain human life before he invented his pressurized airplane cabin. Years later he invented and built an *underwater* balloon that descended to earth's deepest floor, nearly seven miles beneath the surface of the ocean. He did not send others to test out these dangerous inventions, he went himself.

He was neither rich, nor the son of rich parents. During most of his adult life he was under constant financial pressure, needing to raise the money to build and develop inventions that he gave to mankind. Personal gain was never his aim, but to increase man's global range by making available to him the high realms of the stratosphere and the deep realms of the abyssal seas.

Piccard was sixteeen years old when the twentieth century began. He could scarcely have known, at that age, what a role he was to play in the new one. Surely young Auguste never dreamed that his name, and the result of his ideas, would endure through future centuries and help to shape them . . . that he would forge the door to the Space Age and its eventual manned moon-landings, before heading in the opposite direction to give new scope to oceanography, where the answer to the world's future food problem must be found. Surely it never occurred to him that he would earn a permanent place in history as "the man who went both ways."

These amazing feats, and all of the events that were to stem from them, had their origins in an "accident." The accident occurred almost exactly a hundred years before Auguste Piccard was born! That is when the balloon, the simplest form of aircraft, came into being. In a long and intricate chain of circumstances, this was the first link. Eventually it led to Auguste Piccard, and made possible what he achieved.

Toward the end of the eighteenth century Etienne and Jacques Montgolfier, two inventive young French lads, were fooling around in their mother's farmhouse kitchen. One of them held an inverted paper bag, a product manufactured by their father, over the merrily boiling kettle. The bag grew round and taut, and it rose to the ceiling! The boys, fascinated by the idea of flying, were delighted. At eight or nine, Etienne had jumped off the barn roof holding an open umbrella, and landed in a heap bruised but undaunted.

They thought about that floating bag almost constantly for the next year or two while they finished their schooling. Now, in the year 1782, they were ready for a more elaborate experiment. This time they had fashioned their bag from a discarded skirt rescued from the scrap-bag, and they staged their test outdoors. They invited the Mayor and the villagers.

The boys knew that clouds consist of vapor. They reasoned that if they could somehow capture vapor in their bag, the trapped air would make it float, as clouds do. To make vapor they built a fire of damp straw, which let off great billows of smoke, and they suspended their bag above it. It inflated rapidly and rose a thousand feet, descending in a field a mile and a half away.

The boys, watching it waft away higher than their greatest hopes, were wild with joy. They felt sure that their theory was correct, though they couldn't figure out *what had made the bag descend*. They were very sure that it didn't leak. (Later they learned that their theory was not correct. It was not vapor generated by straw combustion that lifted their balloon, but the fact that *air expands when heated*. A given volume of hot air weighs less than its equivalent of cold air. As the air in the balloon cooled it grew heavier, and this is what had forced down the balloon. A century and a half later this fact was to save Auguste Piccard's life.)

The flight's witnesses were flabbergasted. Some

of them leaped on horseback and streaked after the balloon. Word of the boys' achievement spread like a forest fire. They received a royal command from the King of France to stage a demonstration at Versailles the following summer. The boys had taken a long stride from their rural farmhouse kitchen!

When the great day came the Montgolfiers expected to go up in the balloon themselves. The King wouldn't allow them to risk it; he insisted on using animals. That is why King Louis XVI, Marie Antoinette, Benjamin Franklin and the gorgeously dressed members of the royal court watched a duck, a sheep and a rooster rise up in the beautiful balloon *Réveillon*. The balloon was a sight fit for a king. Its exterior bore the royal monogram. A ring of eagles, wings outstretched, had been painted around the base. The balloon came down two miles away, landing its animal passengers safely.

Now the King was eager for a manned flight. He offered to provide a criminal under sentence of death. The King's historian, Pilâtre de Rozier, insisted that no criminal deserved such an honor. He begged the King to be allowed to go himself. Probably the King felt that his court historian

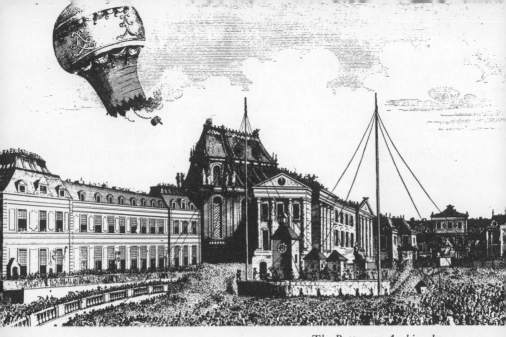

The first ascent of the Montgolfier balloon, *Reveillon*, took place at Versailles in 1783. The passengers for this flight were a duck, a sheep and a rooster.

would be easier to replace than the inventors of the balloon. He consented, and asked the Montgolfiers to construct a suitable balloon, larger than the *Réveillon*. Within a month they had completed the new one. It was sizable enough to carry a man, a fire-pan and enough straw to heat the air in the balloon's bag for a considerable time. At the King's insistence, the balloon was tethered to the ground for this first manned flight. A sponge and a bucket of water were carried along in case the fire got out of control. De Rozier, in this captive flight, stayed aloft for five minutes. A month later he and a member of the royal court made the first free flight and flew over most of Paris. The hot-air balloon was now scientifically accepted, though it still presented an unresolved problem. It would descend when the air inside grew cooler than the surrounding air.

The Montgolfier boys were now famous. They had invented and tested something which no one else had ever thought of. Others seized upon their idea almost immediately, adding improvements. The French physicist Biot once said: "Nothing is so simple as what was invented yesterday. Nothing is so difficult as what remains to be invented tomorrow." Another Frenchman, Jacques Charles, built a balloon which he fueled with *hydrogen* gas, a substance which had been isolated twenty years earlier. (Hydrogen, though highly inflammable, is so much lighter than air that its lifting power is extraordinary.) Jacques and Etienne Montgolfier must have been generous by nature, for they were loud in their praise of Charles and of his clever use of hydrogen. Here was the answer to the problem of descent. Charles's bag was equipped with a valve; the traveler dangling beneath it in the suspended basket had only to jerk a cord leading up

Frightened peasants attack a Montgolfier balloon which landed 15 miles away from its point of departure.

to the balloon to let off gas and begin to descend. The Montgolfiers gave no indication of jealousy or resentment at this modification of their discovery. All that their idea ever earned them was a place in history for having discovered it. Gradually they saw their hot-air balloon give way to the hydrogen balloon.

That first hydrogen balloon took four days to fill and carried no passengers. After climbing about three thousand feet it had drifted to earth nearly fifteen miles away. Frightened peasants had fallen upon it with pitchforks and ripped it to shreds — much as today we might attack a "flying saucer" that landed on our premises. To protect future experiments, the King had to circulate a description of balloons around the countryside.

Four months later Charles and a companion made the first *manned* hydrogen flight. The balloon, equipped with the new escape valve, also carried stones for ballast. These could be heaved overboard to hasten rise. The men carried the first "laboratory" aloft . . . a thermometer and a barometer to measure air pressure and temperature. Everything went well until they landed. Then Charles's companion leaped out, and the balloon, freed of his weight, shot up to nine thousand feet! Charles, having unwillingly become the first hydrogen soloist, yanked on his gas-releasing valve and brought the balloon down quickly before he suffocated.

Now pioneer balloonists sprang up right and left, and ballooning became the rage. Ladies adopted "balloon skirts" and puffed sleeves. Everywhere, small boys experimented with homemade "montgolfiers," much as boys and girls today contrive small rockets. Two early balloonists, Jeffries and Blanchard, made an air crossing of the English Channel. In 1797 another Frenchman made the first parachute jump from a balloon over Paris. Nothing could halt the fad . . . not even the death of De Rozier. The man who, with the

King's permission, had made the very first ascent was killed in a balloon explosion.

Interest spread across the ocean, and François Blanchard went up over Philadelphia, before a large crowd that included George Washington. An early American balloonist often dropped animals from his balloon in parachutes, then allowed his craft to burst and parachuted to safety.

Each year the number of balloon enthusiasts grew, as new uses for balloons were found. During the American Civil War, Thaddeus Lowe sent the first aerial communication. He stretched a wire half a mile long from his balloon to a receiving set in Washington, and telegraphed a message to President Lincoln. Soon afterwards the first aerial photographs were taken. In 1890 the Egyptian pyramids were photographed from above. Long before man conquered Mount Everest, manned free balloons rose to heights that exceeded it. Balloons opened up the atmosphere to scientific investigations, for measuring wind velocity, humidity and temperature. These were the very things that later were to interest Auguste Piccard. But as balloonists attained ever increasing heights, use of *oxygen* became essential, since this was long before the day of Piccard's pressurized cabin. In order to avoid the "bends" (nitrogen bubbles developing in body tissue, known as Caisson Disease) it was necessary to breathe oxygen for hours *before* making an ascent, as well as during the ascent itself. All of these slow and laborious precautions, which often failed, were later to be eliminated by Auguste Piccard's invention.

These eighteenth and nineteenth century events were successive links in a long chain. They led from the balloon's humble farmyard beginning to the twentieth century, when Auguste Piccard was to rise in a balloon which he had modified, to heights deemed impossible for human survival. Then, just as the nineteenth century was drawing to its end, an adventure-tragedy occurred which captured the imagination of the world. Its final chapter was not disclosed for many years, until just before Auguste Piccard set out to conquer the stratosphere. He has told us that it was in his mind on that momentous day!

Early in 1895 a young Frenchman named Salomon Andrée determined to fly over the North Pole in a free balloon. He rigged it with a steering sail to enable it to cut across spiral air currents. On one of his eight test flights he threw down "balloon cards," which were to be returned by the finders with notes telling where they had been picked up, thus helping him to map the balloon's route. (This same idea is often carried out at sea today. Bottles are thrown overboard with messages asking the finder to help establish current drifts by reporting the location where the bottle was picked up.) He developed a "rip valve," enabling him to land at an exact location, and he added guidelines to drag along the ice to reduce his speed. Traveling alone, acting as navigator, observer and photographer, he made more than four hundred observations and covered a thousand miles in his trial flights. He reported to the Academy of Sciences that his balloon could remain aloft for thirty days, that his guide ropes were impregnated with coconut fiber, able to float on water. He and his two companions would be able to develop their aerial photographs in a darkroom built into the balloon's gondola. They would carry sleds, a canvas boat, a tent, arms and ammunition, provisions for four months. Every emergency appeared to have been anticipated, and Andrée's proposed expedition, planned for mid-1897, was endorsed by the Academy of Sciences. Alfred Nobel (inventor of dynamite, and later the donor of the coveted Nobel prizes) became the first contributor to the enterprise. King Oscar of Sweden gave a matching amount, and the rest was quickly raised from the public. Andrée then took the final precaution of testing all the materials sent in by balloon manufacturers for use in his vessel.

Three days after their departure in July 1897 from Bergen, Norway, the carrier pigeons they released brought in the message: "All is well aboard the *Eagle*." The world rejoiced and waited.

That was the last that the nineteenth century ever heard of them! They disappeared as completely as if swallowed up, and no further word came. Extensive sea search was made. The months turned into years, and all hope died of ever knowing what had happened to them. It was assumed that they had either been crushed by an icecap or fallen into the sea.

In 1930, more than a third of a century later, a Norwegian surveying party found the bodies of the three men on a small island two hundred miles from Bergen. Their letters were intact, and their diaries and scientific observations. Even the photographs, taken *thirty-three years earlier*, were unharmed. Their detailed account of their journey included a description of the meals served aboard the *Eagle!* It told of their descent into a sea filled with ice floes where they were constantly forced eastward by open water until at last they reached barren White Island, to die of cold and exhaustion. The journals told an incredibly moving tale of hardship and heroism.

Excitement gripped the world when the Andrée party was found, just one year before Auguste Piccard was to launch his stratospheric balloon. A special expedition was sent to White Island to bring home the bodies of the explorers. A museum was built to house the expedition's relics. The whole story calls to mind Amelia Earhart, the aviatrix who disappeared without a trace in the Pacific during World War II. If she, and her own records and the photographs of her disaster were to turn up today, the same degree of interest would result.

Auguste Piccard was thirteen years old when Andrée vanished, and it made an indelible impression on his mind. Thousands of others were similarly affected, at the end of the nineteenth century when the balloon was the undisputed monarch of the skies. It still serves useful purposes today. But as the twentieth century began, no one could foresee that the balloon's sovereign reign was coming to an end. Its place would soon be usurped by a new invention called an airplane. No one knew that history was going to repeat itself. . . . No one dreamed that, once again, two unknown brothers, Orville and Wilbur Wright, would pave the way!

THESE EIGHTEENTH AND NINETEENTH century events were successive links in the long chain that led to Auguste Piccard. In a giant stride he was to carry ballooning forward to places where no man had ever preceded him.

He and his twin brother Jean were born in Basel, Switzerland, in 1884. It was a wonderful city in which to grow up, for it is located on both banks of the Rhine, where the great river makes a wide curve, and where Switzerland, France and Germany meet. The French Jura Mountains and the German Black Forest are within easy excursion distance. It is landlocked Switzerland's one great inland port. There the boys' father was a physics professor at the ancient University of Basel, founded in the fourteenth century. They lived in a comfortable, happy home, where ideas were considered much more important than money. Scholars and professors frequented the house, and from the time that the twins could sit at the big, round dining-room table, they were exposed to good talk and to probing minds.

They were identical, and had similar interests. They were "mirror" twins, Auguste left-handed and Jean right-handed. Mischievous and high-spirited, they enjoyed confusing their friends, at times even their parents, about their identity. To do this they would often swap names for several days at a time. This was so bewildering that, to tell them apart, their mother sometimes had to give them a task where she could watch their hands. Auguste noticed this, and from an early age began teaching himself to become ambidextrous. Before long he could use both hands at once.

When the twins were not quite six, their father made plans for a family vacation in the Alps. Mountain climbing was his passion, and he wanted to begin training his children at an early age to share it. Paul and Marie, the two older children, were now old enough to start, and the twins could tag along on the lower slopes. There was much dinner-table talk about the proposed holiday.

"Will we be all by ourselves in the mountains, Papa?" asked Jean.

"Certainly not," his father told him. "There are houses all up and down the mountains. No

matter how high we climb, you may be sure we'll see houses perched higher up above us."

Little Jean's eyes popped. "Houses on the mountainside, Papa? How is that possible? The soup would slide off the stove. The children would fall out of bed!" He looked at Auguste and both of them burst out laughing. Even the older children began to giggle. Then Auguste frowned and wrinkled his forehead. He reached in his pocket, pulled out a stubby pencil and began drawing on the fresh tablecloth. *Maman* would scold, but never mind.

"Look here, Jean," he said. "You've got it wrong. You think the houses are tilted, like this, against the mountainsides. I don't think so. I think they will *straddle* the peaks, like this!

Their mother was so delighted at this sign of budding logic that she didn't scold at all. Instead, before washing the tablecloth, she traced off Auguste's childish drawing, and in later years it became a treasured family heirloom which today is in the possession of Auguste Piccard's wife.

The twins were curious and loved to tinker. At nine years old they tried experiments similar to those of the Montgolfiers, also using paper bags filled with hot air. Their father encouraged all

Identical twins, even their mother had difficulty telling them apart. Jean is on the left and Auguste is on the right.

their experiments, even the ones that were dismal failures. "Trial and error," he often told them, "are essential to success."

Both boys were avid readers. Their favorite book was Jules Verne's *Twenty Thousand Leagues Under the Sea*. Auguste, fascinated with the thought of life beneath the sea, often talked about it with his father. Years later, emerging from a bathyscaphe descent, he said he had thought about his childhood's favorite story. "What is impossible in one generation will become commonplace in the next," he told his own children.

On their tenth birthday their mother took the twins to a circus. The major attraction was a tethered balloon where an acrobat performed, dangling by his knees, then by his heels, from the edge of the basket. Jean stayed rooted beneath the balloon but Auguste gave it only a passing glance. He spent the whole morning in front of the lion cage. Long after the lion tamer had finished his act the boy stayed on, gazing at the now-empty round cage where the act had taken place, and at the second cage which surrounded it. In his autobiography, *Earth, Sky and Sea*, he says that at that moment he grasped the principle of the air chamber. He saw that the tamer, by going through a door from the inner to the outer cage, and by closing the first door before opening the second, had penned up the lion very effectively. He had achieved a safe exit for himself. He had also removed the danger of releasing the lion into the crowd. Auguste Piccard states that he still remembered that scene, forty years later. He said that when he built his balloons he mentally substituted the tamer for the ballast, which had to be released without letting the lion, i.e. the air, escape at the same time. Then and there an idea was born in his brain that stuck there half his life, although he had no immediate use for it. Yet it was to surface years later, to help him solve one of the major problems which his sealed cabin presented . . . how to drop ballast from it without letting out the pressurized air upon which the lives of the balloon's occupants depended. Perhaps he was thinking of this childhood experience when he wrote in *Earth, Sky and Sea*: "Each discovery, even the most apparently insignificant one, will end in being of use to man."

When the Piccard twins were nineteen, something occurred which thrilled and changed the world. Orville and Wilbur Wright, two unknown bicycle manufacturers from Dayton, Ohio, flew

120 feet in twelve historic seconds at Kitty Hawk, North Carolina, in a frail, kitelike craft, double-winged, heavier than air, and powered by a gasoline engine. Before noon of that momentous December day in 1903 this first airplane had made three flights. One of them carried its pilot 852 feet in fifty-nine seconds.

A new era was born on that day, but aviation had a long way to go before becoming established, or even useful. Not many persons realized how soon it was to change the range and tempo of their lives, and alter man's concept of distance. At that time it is doubtful if the young Piccards realized it either. At least they, and everyone else, knew that an important door had been opened.

The twins enrolled at the University of Zurich, where Jean majored in chemistry, Auguste in physics and mechanical engineering. Auguste became increasingly interested in meteorology and both twins were deeply interested in balloons, still the only means available to man for the study of the high atmosphere.

Because of their different majors they attended many separate classes, but they continued to meet every day. They had endless discussions on every imaginable subject. One day they fell into a heated discussion over the seven deadly sins. Which one should head the list?

"Greed," said Jean.

"Pride," said Auguste.

Each twin cited cases designed to bolster his own viewpoint, and the argument continued. Finally Jean grew tired of it. "Enough." He shrugged. "There is no way to prove it, so let's drop the subject."

"I'll find a way," vowed Auguste.

Two days later he sought out his brother after classes. "I'm tired of lectures," he said. "Are you ready for some fun? Then listen. Here is what we will do."

A few minutes later Jean walked into the local barber shop. After waiting his turn he sat down in the chair. The barber began cutting his hair and Jean read a book all the while. When the job was finished he looked up.

"Not short enough," he grumbled. "I should have paid attention. Now I must rush off to class, and I suppose you will expect to be paid. But it is robbery! My hair grows so fast that this poor haircut will be useless!" He threw some money on the counter and stalked out past the waiting customers, slamming the door, while the barber glared.

An hour later a shaggy-haired Auguste stormed into the barbershop. "There now, what did I tell you?" he shouted. "And you call yourself a barber! I told you that my hair grows fast. You took my money barely an hour ago, and look at me! Fix it at once. I can't be expected to sit around here all afternoon waiting for you to finish your job."

The barber stared, and so did all the customers. "There, there," said the barber hastily. "No need to shout. I'll get it short enough this time. It seems to me that you should visit a *doctor* as well as a barber!"

Auguste submitted to the haircut, then stood up. "I paid you for the first poor job," he declared. "You'll get no more from me." He stalked out.

Ten minutes later both boys walked into the shop together. Auguste, smiling broadly, stretched out the money for the second haircut. "Here you are, my friend," he said. "A joke's a joke, isn't it?"

But the barber was white with anger. He thrust aside the money and grabbed up his scissors. "Out of my shop before I call the police, you two!" he shouted. "You'd make a fool of an honest, hardworking man! And before my customers, too!"

He lunged at them, even pursued them out of the door.

Auguste and Jean ran out and raced around a corner a full block away. There they flopped on a bench, breathing hard.

"Whew!" Jean mopped his forehead. "Who would have thought he'd get so angry? He didn't even take his money. He only wanted to wring our necks!"

"He thinks we made him look ridiculous," said Auguste, "and that made him forget all about the money. Isn't that what I've been telling you? Now will you admit that pride is stronger than greed?"

Jean stared at him. "What! Did you dream up this silly prank just to settle an argument we had two whole days ago?"

"Two days, or two years, what does it matter? I tell you, Jean, *I had to find out!*"

While the Piccards were still in college both of them obtained their licenses as free-balloon pilots, and made a number of flights. In 1913 they made a sixteen-hour flight together, to measure temperature and density inside a balloon. They served a time in the Swiss Army's Balloon Corps. Too tall and too thin to meet the regulations for active duty, the Piccard twins were used as civilian technicians. In those days all major countries had Balloon Corps as part of their standing armies.

During our own Civil War the Union forces observed the Confederate armies from balloons, and also sent telegraphic messages to headquarters from aloft. In World War II balloons again proved useful. In London captive balloons provided barriers against low-flying enemy aircraft, and the British Navy used free balloons to help locate German submarines.

Now for the first time the Piccard twins separated, not knowing that it was to be for a lifetime, though they met many times over the years, even engaged in short-term business ventures together. Jean went to Boston to teach at Massachusetts Institute of Technology. Later he was to marry an American girl and become an American citizen. Auguste stayed behind. First, he became professor of physics at the University of Zurich, then shortly after at the University of Brussels. He continued his studies of meteorology on the side. For this he needed a balloon, but he could not possibly afford to buy one.

Luck was with him. Swiss sportsmen had formed the Swiss Aero Club. Its members, interested in transoceanic balloon racing, had set their sights on the James Gordon Bennett Trophy. This annual prize was given by the imaginative publisher of the New York *Herald* (the same man who had sent his reporter Stanley into the middle of darkest Africa to seek out Livingstone). Many countries competed fiercely for the trophy. The competition was a highly sporting event, for once a balloon becomes airborne it goes where the wind blows. Learning to "play the winds" required a high degree of skill. Piccard persuaded the Swiss Aero Club members to let him use the club's equipment for flights with scientific objectives. He made many such flights. He invented a machine for measuring the temperature of gas within a balloon. The generosity of the Swiss sportsmen allowed him to acquire familiarity with the balloon long before he dreamed of taking one up into the stratosphere.

Grateful to the Swiss Aero Club, he agreed to pilot one Bennett Trophy flight for them. In the early twenties, shortly after his marriage, he entered the race. The takeoff from Brussels was at dusk, and in almost no time he was flying over Basel. He peered out of the gondola and saw that

27

he could recognize the streets of the city where he had grown up. He flew lower, spotted his mother's house, and saw that her bedroom window was open. He yelled out her name over and over as he flew past. (The next morning his mother, who knew that he was competing in the Bennett Race, mentioned at breakfast that she was afraid some disaster had overtaken him. She had, she vowed, heard his voice during the night, calling out to her "from heaven.") Auguste was never able to persuade her that it was his actual voice she had heard. She continued to think that it was a premonition of impending danger, for only a few minutes after Auguste's balloon sailed over Basel, a severe electrical storm struck. Three of the competing balloons were hit by lightning, and two of the pilots were killed.

Piccard brought his own balloon down only about one hundred kilometers from the starting point, which disqualified him in the competition. He felt that weather conditions made the risk too great for a nonscientific venture. But the experience was not wasted; the following year he published a paper suggesting ways to minimize danger from lightning in future balloon construction. There was an additional result. His speedy withdrawal from the race convinced his bride that he would never take foolhardy risks, and from then on she had absolute faith in his professional judgment. In years to come, she was to need it!

Increasingly, Piccard became interested in *cosmic rays*. These ultrastrong rays contain particles of energy greater than those of any other known source. Cosmic ray research was becoming one of the most important fields of physics. Piccard figured that he would need to go up ten miles. He wanted to observe the rays in mass, before they had become somewhat dispersed by colliding with molecules from earth's atmosphere. This would mean going up into the *stratosphere*, which begins seven and a half miles above sea level, and which Piccard called "the region of perpetual good weather." No such flight had ever been made successfully, with passengers aboard. Unmanned "sounding balloons," lighter because they carried only instruments, had been sent up into the stratosphere. Such a balloon had gone up from Hamburg, Germany, in 1930, reaching an altitude of nearly twenty-two miles, and its instruments showed a temperature at that height of -60 degrees Fahrenheit, with air pressure at $1/250$ of pressure at sea level. No human being could survive under such conditions without oxygen. Several balloonists, carrying oxygen, had made stratospheric attempts, and had lost consciousness. On one flight by a United States Navy captain, instruments showed that record heights had been achieved, but the pilot was dead on descent. This was a discouraging prospect. Also Piccard's plans required an especially light balloon, for he wanted to carry aloft a well-equipped science laboratory. He concluded that his plans could only be carried out in a *pressurized cabin*, something then unheard of. This meant that he would have to build it himself.

He was deeply interested, but he had no money to build such a craft. He might never have gotten around to doing anything about it if he hadn't been nudged from another direction . . . his interest in airplanes and his now-fervent belief in their future — a belief that was by no means universally shared.

All through the 1920s, aviation had been surging ahead. This was the era of the daring "barnstormer" pilots who performed at airshows before gaping crowds, and of the early aviation explorers. In 1926 Commander Richard Evelyn Byrd flew from Norway to the North Pole and back. Three years later he dropped the United States flag on top of the South Pole. A regularly scheduled flight from New York to Los Angeles was begun in 1930. The trip, carrying only a handful of passengers, required thirty-nine hours, for there was an overnight stop in Kansas City, and twelve stops en route, for fueling purposes. Few persons had ever flown; those who had were apt to boast about it. "I've been up in an airplane," was a statement that would evoke a stream of interested questions at any gathering. The public still didn't take aviation seriously, in spite of its pride in Lindbergh's 1927 transatlantic flight. (An airplane trip in those days was a far cry from today's luxurious experience, where almost no motion is felt, delicious meals are served, and movies often shown.) At that time airplanes were small, dangerous and uncomfortable. The pressure on eardrums was severe. Passengers with a head cold or any kind of ear disturbance were advised not to fly.

Piccard believed that many of these problems could be solved if only the air services could be persuaded to use the high stratosphere. He reasoned that the lessened resistance of the rarefied air would make flights smoother and high speeds possible. The time needed for long trips could be greatly reduced. The world would be drawn closer together.

He talked to specialists, suggesting an *airtight cabin*, to offset the low stratospheric pressure that made human survival impossible. The authorities laughed at his suggestion. The reason given was that it had never been done before. As a scientist, Piccard found such a reason intolerable. If this kind of reasoning were to prevail, the course of human progress would come to a standstill. If aviation's experts wouldn't build an airtight cabin, he would do it himself. He would prove his theory. Not in an airplane, for he was no aviator, but in a balloon.

Suppose for a moment that Alan Shepard and the first astronauts had had to *invent* their space capsule, find ways to finance it, then build it themselves. The notion seems impossible. Yet this is exactly what the far-from-wealthy university professor Auguste Piccard had to do, both with his stratospheric balloon and later with his underwater balloon, or bathyscaphe. Under these conditions it is almost a miracle that either one of them ever came into being.

But Auguste Piccard was a determined man. He

made up his mind that somehow he was going to achieve that miracle. He didn't exactly know how he was going to do it, but the way to begin was to take one step at a time. "Trial and error are essential to success." . . . Wasn't that what his father had told him so many years ago?

IN 1931 Auguste Piccard, happily married to one of his former students and the father of five children, was about to launch his stratospheric balloon. There was no demand for such a thing, and its building and launching aroused little interest. It was the result of dogged determination.

What did this iron-willed man look like? He had a prominent Adam's apple and his nearsighted eyes peered out through double-thick spectacles. His long straggling hair, sticking out in wisps beneath his Basque beret, was beginning to thin out a little on top. In appearance at least, Auguste Piccard was the very embodiment of the Absent-Minded Professor. His total powers of concentration on his current projects usually made him unaware of his surroundings. His poor eyesight gave him a lost, gentle look. As he wandered down the street, deep in thought, his students usually assumed that Madame Piccard must have tucked a handful of small change and a clean handkerchief in his pocket, and reminded him to eat. Everyone sensed his dependence on her, a motherly, sensible woman with a quiet charm and a ready smile, endlessly busy with the demands of her home and her large brood, not to mention those of a husband who needed her in many of the same ways her children did. They knew that she was proud of him and encouraged him in all his dreams — perhaps without fully understanding them, for few persons did, but wholeheartedly and selflessly — all the more because their only son Jacques's interests were cast in the same mold.

"Jacques is so brilliant and so good," she often remarked. "He will do great things in his own name. But there is a certain spark of creative genius that belongs exclusively to his father!"

His students told endless stories about Auguste Piccard, but the stories were always slanted kindly, for he was a great favorite on the university campus. They relished the way he would stride up to the blackboard, make mechanical drawings with both hands at once, then turn on them suddenly and say, "The Lord gave you two hands and a brain. Why don't you use them all?" In a strange way his students felt protective toward him, for he seemed so totally unworldly. Once a student, encountering him on a narrow campus path, stepped aside to let him pass. They exchanged a few words.

"Which way was I walking when I met you, young man?" asked Piccard.

"Why, that way, sir." The student pointed toward the lecture hall.

"Good. Then that means I must have eaten my lunch." Piccard nodded and continued on, seemingly unaware that another Piccard story was about to circulate the campus!

How had Auguste Piccard, outwardly a dreamer, managed to raise the huge amount of money needed to build his stratospheric balloon? Luckily for him, King Albert I of Belgium had just founded the Belgian National Fund for Scientific Research (*Fonds Nationales Belge de la Recherche Scientifique*), and the Belgians were keenly interested in ballooning. All over the tiny country there was rejoicing because Belgium had just won permanent possession of the Bennett Trophy for transatlantic balloon racing, by capturing it for three successive years. The King knew that his subjects would approve of using their national scientific funds for a balloon project, and he gave Piccard the money, as a grant. Piccard, with a scientist's detachment, called his revolutionary new balloon the *FNSR*, in honor of the Fund that had supplied him with the money. It never crossed his mind to name it for himself. He found recreation and challenge in putting his ideas to use and in testing out his theories. He did his work with zest and joy.

Piccard's balloon had to be unusually large and light. In its airtight cabin it must lift the men and their instruments off the ground, and then carry them up into the stratosphere, where each cubic yard of gas supports only one-tenth as much as it does down on earth. Unlike other existing balloons, it was to be only partially gas-filled at the start, to keep it light at the takeoff. The gas, in the course of the climb, would expand under the decreasing atmospheric pressure, and the balloon would round out into full spherical form when it reached the stratosphere. These reasons had compelled Piccard to build a balloon vastly different from the standard balloons of the day. He chose Augsberg, Germany, for his takeoff because the town was distant from the sea in all directions. It was Madame Piccard who urged this place of departure. She felt that it minimized the risk of hav-

Auguste Piccard's hermetically sealed cabin was the first step in the development of the pressurized cabin.

ing to make a landing on water. Except for this one request, she kept silent about any fears she may have had.

Instead of the conventional basket, Piccard's balloon had a hermetically sealed cabin that hung below the gasbag, and on this cabin the very lives of the balloon's operators depended. The expression "vanish into thin air" is based on the fact that, as we rise to great heights, the air *does* become thinner for the reason that there is less of it pressing down from on top. (By the same token, the deeper we go underwater, the more the pressure *increases*, because there is more water on top of us and above the water that surrounds us.) *FNSR*'s cabin was made of light, strong thin sheets of aluminum, and the two observers peered out past their instruments through eight portholes. These were forged from two sheets of glass separated by a slight layer of air, giving the windows thermal insulation, and preventing them from breaking under pressure. They did not even frost over in the —70-degree Fahrenheit temperature of the stratosphere!

Now came the big problem . . . how to drop ballast, necessary to hasten rise, from the sealed cabin without letting off lifesaving air. It was at this moment that Auguste Piccard put into use the air chamber, whose principle he had grasped so many years ago on his tenth birthday, in front of the lion cage. The lead-shot ballast was poured via funnel into the container through an upper cock, and *that cock was closed*. This retained the cabin's air (which Piccard thought of as the lion). *Then* a second cock was opened from the container, and from it the ballast was dumped outside. His parallel with the lion tamer was indeed exact.

At last, on May 26, 1931, Auguste Piccard and his companion Paul Kipfer were ready for their takeoff from Augsberg. Today's astronauts would sympathize with them. Forecasts were favorable, the balloon was inflated with 100,000 cubic feet of hydrogen, and the two men climbed aboard. In today's words, the countdown had started. Then the weather changed abruptly and the winds became so violent that the two men were forced to come out and the balloon had to be emptied: but not before it had been badly knocked about, with consequences they were to feel at a later moment.

The next morning was calm, and once again Piccard and Kipfer reinflated the balloon, went back into the cabin and closed the porthole behind them. Again the wind rose, and the men expected another postponement. Then, glancing through a porthole, they saw that they were skimming over the city's roofs and chimneys. The ground crew had released the balloon without signaling to the men inside their cabin! So began, in an awkward and amateurish way, the most historic balloon flight

Auguste Piccard prepares to take off into the stratosphere.

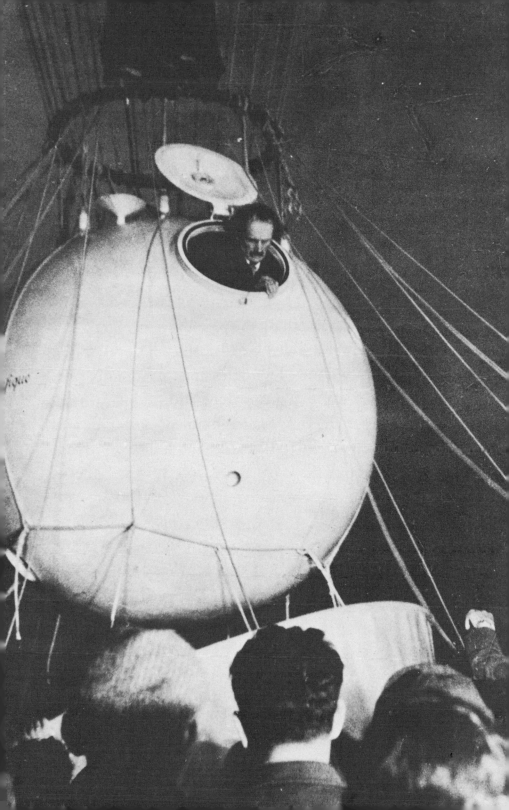

since De Rozier's voyage in the Montgolfiers' balloon 150 years earlier.

Up shot the balloon. Within moments Piccard heard an ominous whistling sound. An electrical instrument which pierced the cabin's walls had been broken off by the balloon's earlier tossing in the wind, and somehow this had escaped notice. Now it was leaking out vital air. Piccard began plugging and patching the hole with Vaseline and insulating tape. His concern increased when Kipfer, who was watching the pressure gauge, reported that the pressure was equal inside and outside the cabin, at two and a half miles up in the thinning air. This was critical. Danger of suffocation was increasing with every passing moment, and there was not much time left. Piccard, who still believed that he could pull the valve and descend at the last possible moment, continued working as calmly and unhurriedly as if he'd been in his workshop at home. Soon he managed to halt the air leak. The pressure had gone down so alarmingly, however, that he had to pour small quantities of liquid oxygen on the floor, knowing that its evaporation would increase the pressure inside the cabin.

Now, twenty-five minutes after leaving the ground, they had reached the stratosphere and were *nine miles up!* The balloon, which on takeoff had been shaped something like an inverted pear, was now round and taut from the expansion of gas inside it. The emergency was over and Piccard and Kipfer had time to look about them. What they saw was breathtaking. At the horizon they could see where the sharply defined lines of the stratosphere and troposphere met. They peered down the jagged crests of the Bavarian Alps, and at the approaching Tyrol, far beneath them. They threw out ballast and rose even higher.

They had done it! They had proved that survival in an airtight cabin was possible in the stratosphere, and they were triumphant. Now they began to think about coming down. This was a simple procedure. All it required was a jerk, to open the gas-release valve. But the comedy of errors which had begun with the morning's impromptu takeoff was not over yet. *The valve was jammed. . . .*

It was far worse than merely being trapped in the sky. They were stranded in the *stratosphere!*

IF EVER THERE was a moment of justifiable panic, this was it. Auguste Piccard and Paul Kipfer were wafting around nearly ten miles above the earth with a rapidly diminishing supply of oxygen, in a cabin with a crudely patched-up hole that might give way at any moment, bringing them quick suffocation. The men kept their heads. There were too many problems calling for their immediate attention.

They had planned a noon landing, but as a precaution they had brought along enough oxygen to last until sunset in the airtight cabin. But soon after Piccard's emergency repair job on the valve they began hearing another faint whistle around the air-hole, and the air loss was confirmed by the aching in their ears. To make matters worse, the balloon's drift indicator showed they were headed toward the Adriatic Sea, though rather slowly. This gave them hope that they would not reach open sea before nightfall. They knew that when the sun began to set the balloon's gas would cool, causing them to drop rapidly . . . perhaps rapidly enough to get below the stratosphere's thin air. This, their only hope, was hours away, and even if their oxygen held out and the airhole didn't spread, there was now the added risk that they might fall into the sea.

As if these problems weren't enough, another one developed. A sudden lurch broke one of the mercury barometers and the liquid metal spilled out on the cabin floor. They had to get rid of it in a hurry, before the mercury ate a hole in the aluminum floor, but they had no pump aboard. They did locate a small length of tubing, and by putting one end in a puddle on the floor, and thrusting the other out of the airhole, they sucked the mercury out into the vastness of the stratosphere. One problem had been conquered!

But as fast as they disposed of a problem, another rose to take its place. Now they began to experience severe weather changes. Earlier in the morning the cabin's inside walls had been covered with frost, as they traveled rapidly through the intense stratospheric cold of around seventy degrees below zero. This frost, which had made their teeth chatter, now became a blessing; as the fierce sun of the stratosphere, with an intensity twice that of sea level, struck the aluminum cabin, the heat inside rose to over a hundred degrees, and the melting particles of frost *snowed* down on them. They grew desperately thirsty in the intense heat, and they drank all their water. Then they hit on the idea of licking the melting frost as it seeped down the cabin walls. Another problem had been overcome.

At two o'clock the sun had passed its zenith and they began a slow descent. It was *too* slow. Calculations showed that at this rate their oxygen would never hold out. At three o'clock the speed of descent increased, but not fast enough to save them, for they were still in the stratosphere, dependent upon their emergency oxygen. Piccard and Kipfer decided not to make a single unnecessary move that might increase their rate of breathing. They sat motionless, in total silence. There wasn't much to say. Between them, like an almost tangible thing, lay the certain knowledge that this would either be the most important day of their lives or the final one. Only time would tell the story, and it stretched like an eternity before them.

Piccard found himself thinking about Salomon Andrée, the young Frenchman who had set out in

1897 to fly across the North Pole in a balloon, and who had vanished without a trace until 1930 when a Norwegian fishing expedition had found his remains on a lonely, ice-bound island. Piccard began to wonder if the *FNRS* and its occupants would ever be found. A scientist first and foremost, he wished that they had had time to write down their observations and to take photographs as André had done.

By six o'clock the oxygen supply was almost exhausted, but joy of joys, the sun was sinking! The balloon grew colder and its speed of descent increased. Now it was truly a race for time. At eight o'clock when their oxygen was nearly gone and they were beginning to yawn and grow light-headed, the altimeter showed seven and a half miles above the earth. In moments they were below the stratosphere, able to breathe earth's air. Via a tap they slowly decreased the cabin's pressure. Now they were below the clouds and it was safe to move about. They rushed to the portholes to find out where they were. Beneath them they saw a winding river and a valley, and not, as they had feared, the Adriatic Sea.

They must have thought that their troubles were over at last. Then Piccard realized that the broken escape valve was going to cause them more trouble. This time it would be a landing problem. They were going to need to throw out more ballast, to stabilize the balloon and to avoid a very hard landing. If only the jammed valve were functioning, they could have heaved out ballast somewhat recklessly. Without the escape valve to let off gas they couldn't do this. They were afraid that dumping ballast would shoot them back up into the stratosphere in their now-depressurized cabin. It was too big a risk.

There was only one thing to do. They had to chance the hard landing. They dumped out only a tiny bit of ballast, to lessen the shock of the hard impact with the ground, and braced themselves for what was to come.

Well after dark, and at 15,000 feet, when the air pressure had equalized inside and outside the cabin, Piccard and Kipfer opened the manhole and gulped in fresh air. They had survived seventeen hazardous hours, but what good would that do them if they couldn't make a safe landing?

They took their bearings and got a terrible shock. The biggest problem of all was staring them in the face. In the distance well ahead of them they could see the dark and forbidding outlines of mountains *whose peaks reached up above them!* It looked as if fate had played a cruel joke on them and brought them safely down from the stratosphere just in time to collide with a mountain. At that moment they bumped on an ice field and bounced off again, flying over a glacier, its yawning crevices clearly visible in the moonlight, savagely beautiful. This was no place to land. They whisked over a village and flashed a torch as they sped by. The fearsome walls of the mountainside seemed to be rushing at them when suddenly they flew over a tiny open plateau. Quickly, before they had left it behind, they fumbled with the balloon's ripping panel and jerked the cord. The balloon emptied as if it had been punctured. They dropped straight down on the snow covered ice, badly jarred and shaken up, but saved from real injury by the cushioning effect of the deep snow. Then they took stock. The cabin floor was strewn with instruments . . . bags of ballast were topsy-turvy and the balloon's empty envelope was flapping ghostlike in the cutting wind. But they had made it back to earth safe and sound, and nothing else seemed to matter. Surely they could manage not to freeze to death, and to get back to civilization somehow, when daylight made it safe to travel. After what they had been through, these seemed minor problems. They had no idea where they were. The balloon's altimeter showed that they were 8700 feet above sea level, but they had no way of knowing in what chain of mountains. They were too exhausted to care.

Somehow, wrapped in the balloon's close-woven fabric, they survived the night. Every few minutes they jumped up and down and flayed each other with their hands, to keep up circulation. Later, Professor Piccard was to tell the reporters, jokingly, that this was the hardest part of their stratospheric trip. At dawn they tied themselves to-

Threatening mountain peaks greet Auguste Piccard as he is forced to land in this desolate area.

Madame Auguste Piccard

gether with a double rope and inched their way cautiously down the mountain. Each step of the way they tested the snow for depth, using a long stick extracted from the balloon's rigging. In this slow way they worked their way down toward the village, and at noon they were met by a party of skiers from the village over which they had flashed their signal the night before. Forty of the rescuers went all the way back to their landing point, following their tracks, and carried out the *FNSR*'s envelope, returning the gasbag to the village unripped and unharmed. So ended history's first successful stratospheric flight.

The small cabin lies empty on its landing sight, surrounded by mountains.

Madame Auguste Piccard

But what had been going on at home all this time? As the hours went on, and the expected landing time came and went, hope for the two explorers faded. No one had reported sighting the balloon. Newspaper extras hit the streets all over the world, in a variety of languages. "Death Feared for Occupants of Piccard Balloon. . . . Oxygen Supply Exhausted. . . ." All over the world people thought about the ungainly, abstracted professor, so often the subject of caricature, with warm and fervent hopes; and about his wife and all those little children. Reporters displayed the sensitivity to leave the supposed "widow" alone, but over in America they swarmed around Jean Piccard, besieging him with questions. What did he figure had gone wrong? Did he think that the balloon would ever be found, so that the men's fate could be confirmed and the mechanical difficulties established? But Jean refused to voice despair. Auguste was ingenious, he could overcome all sorts of problems . . . it was too soon to abandon hope.

"Besides," he said, "if Auguste were dead, *I would know it!*"

All these years the brothers had met occasionally, even though their lives had taken different turns. Yet experience, which has a way of marking men's countenances, had kept theirs as identical as ever. The reporters, looking at Auguste Piccard's exact duplicate, took hope from his assurance.

When Piccard and Kipfer finally reached civilization, they looked astonishingly fresh. Piccard's first act was to send a telegram to his wife. Then he sent another one, to the workmen at the factory where the balloon had been built. "The balloon was so well constructed that I couldn't make it come down any sooner." He was so happy that his joy almost bubbled. The quiet, contained professor told the reporters glowing details about the astonishing blue of the high atmosphere, and the vast additional brilliance of the moon, when viewed from the stratosphere.

In Zurich the Swiss Aero Club gave Piccard and Kipfer a hero's welcome and also gave them the official word that they had set a new world's altitude record. A few days later Piccard's students at the University of Brussels carried their physics professor in triumph on their shoulders, ringing cowbells and shouting themselves hoarse.

For the rest of the world, Piccard's safe return was cause for rejoicing, but his enthusiasm over the success of his flight was not shared. Few persons seemed to feel that Piccard, by doing what he had set out to do, had proved his theory. To them, the feasibility of the airtight cabin was far from established. Newspapers did not accord the same amount of coverage to man's conquest of the stratosphere that they gave, years later, to Hillary's climb to the top of Mount Everest. Yet Piccard's was a scientific advance, while Hillary's was a feat of endurance. The press did not play up Piccard's achievement, or his contribution to science. Instead, it wrote about the difficulties he had encountered, and his "luck" in surviving them. No airplane manufacturers rushed into the production of pressurized cabins. No other stratospheric balloons were proposed. Clearly, since nobody else was going to do it, Auguste Piccard would have to make a *second* flight!

The following year, this time with the financial backing of his only "fans," the members of the Swiss Aero Club, Piccard made a second trip to the stratosphere in the *FNSR*. A huge crowd saw him off, late in August of 1932, at early dawn, and many of them felt that he was pushing his luck. They were never to forget the sight . . . the balloon straining at its ropes, the tall, stork-thin Professor Piccard thrusting his long neck out of the manhole, waving to his wife and children and to hordes of

Madame Auguste Piccard

Preparation for the second flight goes on through the night.

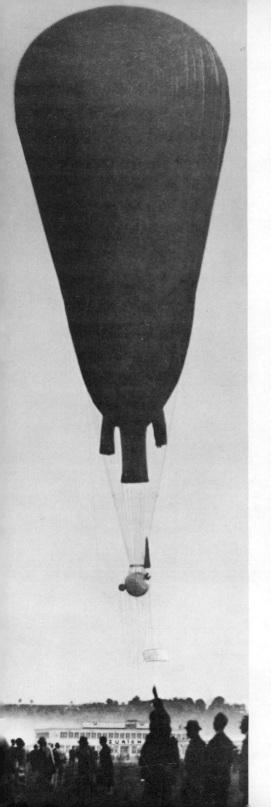

friends and students who had forgathered, hearts in their throats. Then Piccard gave the signal for the takeoff, and pulled his head in like a turtle drawing back into its shell. The balloon seemed to shudder, then rose quickly while the crowd roared. Soon it was only a tiny speck, black against a skyline streaked with dawn.

The flight was successful from the outset. It was as if all the troubles had been lumped into that first, plague-ridden test flight. This one was uneventful. It not only set a new world record, topping the one made in the first flight the preceding year, but it established the airtight cabin in ballooning and in aviation. Work was immedi-

The balloon takes off at dawn.
Madame Auguste Piccard

ately begun on six larger stratospheric balloons, one in Poland, two in Russia and three in the United States.

The aviation industry, which had unknowingly helped to lure Piccard into his stratospheric venture, took a bit longer to bow to the trend. At the end of 1933, Piccard's stratospheric gondola was still the only pressurized aircraft cabin in existence. It was not until July 1940, nine years after the first Piccard achievement, that TWA, with a Boeing Constellation, flew the first *commercial* stratoliner. Years after his father's death, Jacques Piccard was to remark, "I never step across the threshold of a modern airplane's cabin without remembering that my father invented the first one."

But what about Auguste Piccard on that day back in 1932 when his second stratospheric flight with its newest altitude record had been completed? He might have been expected to challenge the succession of aeronauts who soon broke his record and ran up new ones. [Within a year Auguste Piccard's twin brother Jean established a new world record in America, in a stratospheric balloon.] Auguste Piccard did not choose to try.

As soon as he had safely landed, Madame Piccard

put her foot down. *No more stratospheric flights.* By nature quick and extremely active, she had made dozens of trips to distant balloon fields over the years, arriving at dawn, only to find that winds had erased the schedule and that the balloon was not even inflated. This kind of thing she had taken in her stride, but these two stratospheric flights were something else again! She had five children and a husband who was no longer young. He was as lean and lanky as a pole bean, too abstracted to care what he ate, or when. If an accident ever shattered his strong eyeglasses, he'd be helpless. Hadn't he done enough, in inventing the stratospheric balloon and then making that nightmarish test flight? One day his luck would run out. Surely it was time for younger men to carry on, using the tool he had created for them. She had had enough sleepless nights, worrying about her husband's safety. Enough was enough! She spoke her piece, then braced herself for his expected protests, determined to stand firm.

But wonder of wonders, her husband made no objection. He agreed readily, almost meekly. It is easy to imagine her saying to her children, "Your dear papa is coming to his senses at last. Perhaps he realizes that he's not getting any younger. We must put our heads together and find a hobby for him."

The children's dear papa, however, was giving no thought to the matter of his age. Another idea, one that he had filed away in his mind years ago, had taken hold of him. Far from hugging his world altitude record to himself, he *wanted* others to top it, and the sooner the better, for this would hasten the day when aviation would finally dare to make use of the stratosphere. That was what he had set out to accomplish, and any world records picked up along the way were merely incidental. He had other plans! Madame Piccard, unfortunately, was not going to care much for his new "hobby." Right now, he felt sure, was the very moment to develop something that would be infinitely more dangerous, infinitely more slow and difficult and expensive to create and test and perfect than anything he had yet attempted. . . . He was going to challenge the sea, earth's last frontier, in an *underwater* balloon.

IF, THROUGH COUNTLESS ages past, man had cast yearning glances toward the unknown skies, we may be sure that he had looked with calculation at the familiar sea. Here was something tangible that he could see and touch, from which he derived sustenance and a source of livelihood. He knew and feared her many moods, her tidal waves, and the fearful storms that washed sperm whales and other monstrous creatures of the deep upon her beaches. He had used hollowed logs and dugouts to range her coasts, then learned to harness the wind for longer journeys. He had free-dived, to rob her of her coral and her pearls, and had fashioned nets to haul in her infinite varieties of food. The sea was at once his enemy and his friend. But what lay within and beneath her at the great depths? How could he, a creature without gills, find out?

Primitive man had no scientific understanding of depth pressure. He did not know that it doubles at the first thirty-three feet of descent, then increases at the rate of fifteen pounds each additional fifteen feet below the surface. He had found to his sorrow, though, that there were limits beyond which he could not dive safely. He had suffered hemorrhages of the nose, ears and mouth after surfacing from free dives. He had devised clever methods to enable him to stay below the surface beyond his breathing span. The snorkel was anticipated centuries ago, when men carrying hollow reeds in their mouths were able to remain a few feet below the surface and swim around freely. Other men hugged heavy stones to hasten descent while they held their breath. Mother-of-pearl, for whose shells it is necessary to dive, has been excavated from diggings that archeologists date at 4500 D.C. The Roman naturalist Pliny (A D 23–79) has written about dives for pen-shells; these are a species of clams whose long bronze strands, finer than silk, provided the thread for antiquity's finest raiment, cloth-of-gold. There is a medieval French print in the Museum of Cluny which shows Alexander the Great seated cross-legged in a glass barrel which was suspended, like William Beebe's in the 1930s, from a surface vessel. Aristotle gives an account of this same descent. We also know that the Greeks and Romans used sponges, which had to be extracted from the sea. Within the narrow limits of his knowledge and his existing means, early man did his best to penetrate this alien territory.

No great strides in underwater descent were made until the seventeenth century. Then Edmund Halley, the astronomer who discovered the comet that bears his name and comes within earth's range once every seventy-five years, became interested in an underwater treasure salvage. In 1691 this gifted man contrived a diving bell and went down sixty feet. He stayed there for two hours. His homemade contraption hung from the boom of a surface ship, from which it was lowered into the sea by chains and pulleys. Air was supplied to the divers in ironbound casks, each containing around four gallons of compressed air. The casks, after being lowered, were pulled *under* the bell, where the men opened them, then sent them back to the surface to be refilled. It was an ingenious device for a dive of limited depth.

As for the ultradepths, which cover about half the earth, and which have been dark since the world began, no one seriously believed they could be reached, or that marine life could exist there. Then toward the end of our American Civil War a professor of natural history at Edinburgh ventured out on the first oceangoing vessel equipped for deep-sea research. Charles Wyville Thomson, on the HMS *Challenger*, caused genuine scientific excitement by dredging up an abundance of marine life at greater depths than had ever been found before. Here was conclusive proof that marine life could exist in the great pressures of the ocean's abyssal depths, and in its total darkness.

The *Challenger*'s globe-circling expedition lasted three and a half years, and its rich haul of scientific material took years to evaluate. Hundreds of unknown species of undersea life were discovered on the voyage. Some creatures were able to send out powerful rays of light which they could turn on or off at will, presumably to help them seek out their prey. Others had long feelers for groping their way around in the inky dark. Once the crew hauled up a giant squid, whose huge sinuous tentacles writhed and twisted like boa constrictors. Nearby they ran across a dying whale and towed it ashore. Its vast body was covered with round marks imprinted there by the squid's suckers. It was easy for them to visualize the terrifying battle that had taken place between these monsters, miles beneath the calm surface of the sea. It was a picture they did not like to dwell upon, and that made them glad of the sturdy planks beneath their feet.

The scientists were constantly hauling up sediment from the bottom, to study and analyze. Samples showed the ocean floor carpeted with a deep layer of ooze, the result of a "rain" of dead organisms from the heavily populated middle regions of the sea. Over and over again the men found the same varieties of marine specimen, in a wide geographical area. They proved that it is water *temperature*, not location, that determines marine habitat. Charles Wyville Thomson was knighted for his immense contribution to oceanography.

It was exciting to find these strange forms of life. But all of them, and the later ones brought to his own oceanographic museum by Prince Albert of Monaco, were *hauled up to the surface* by trawls or dredges. The scientists viewed them from shipboard, high and dry. It did not occur to them that men would soon be able to go down to the great depths, and that the day was fast coming when these wonders could be observed in their own natural surroundings.

It took World War II to provide a breakthrough. That is when *sonic sounding* was perfected. A sound was bounced off the ocean floor

and its return was timed, making it possible to esti-
mate depth accurately in fathoms. (A fathom is
six feet.) This method soon replaced the miles of
heavy cable once used for depth measurements.
Not only that, but these sonic "spyglasses" showed
that the ocean bottom, far from being a flat and
monotonous plain, was studded with great mountain ranges and volcanoes, as well as swift undersea
rivers; it was split with trenches and huge crevices,
some deeper than the Grand Canyon. The deepest
of all the trenches, the Marianas Trench not far
from Guam, was located by the *Challenger* on a
mapping voyage and appropriately dubbed "the
Challenger Deep" — 35,800 feet straight down.
This was indeed the deepest known place on earth!

But could man ever reach this vast, sunless world
of endless night, and return to tell the tale? It
seemed unlikely. Then in 1930, while Auguste
Piccard's mind was occupied with the task of perfecting his stratospheric balloon for an altitude
record, William Beebe and his engineer Otis Barton established a new depth record. They penetrated below the surface of the ocean more than
half a mile, in a steel globe hung to a cable, called a
bathysphere. This was an epic achievement. Until
then oceanographers had been confined to the

ocean's surface. Now they could go to the very depth they were investigating.

Many persons rushed to their libraries to reread Jules Verne's *Twenty Thousand Leagues Under the Sea*. Somehow the story no longer seemed implausible. Beebe forced the public to revise its opinion of what is possible for man-beneath-the-sea, just as today's astronauts have given us second thoughts about what was once termed "space fiction." Beebe's name became a household word.

No one admired his accomplishments more than Auguste Piccard, or was more generous in his praise of it. But Beebe's journey had come to an end about six and a half miles from the ultrabottom, and that was where Auguste Piccard had set his sights.

He had already opened one scientific frontier by going *up* ten miles. He had hardly landed when he made up his mind that he wanted to go *down* seven miles and open up another. He had reason to believe that the same scientific principles would apply, in a sort of reverse process. In this he was to prove correct, but the additional difficulties were beyond his power to imagine. He was to discover them laboriously and painfully as he went along, and learn to overcome them. . . .

2

THE CASUAL OBSERVER will see in the stratospheric balloon and the deep-sea submersible, two objects as diametrically opposite as the direction in which each is headed. Piccard was struck by the similarities between them and by the many identical construction problems that they posed. But it was not a case of seeing a parallel to his balloon that led him to his new venture. It was the other way around. He had thought of his undersea vessel first, while still a student at the University of Zurich. This was years before a stratospheric flight had ever occurred to him, and long before he had any notion of the problems the idea would pose, or the knowledge to resolve them. Later, he had picked a name for his imaginary craft . . . bathy*scaphe*, from the Greek (*bathy* — deep; *skaphe* — vessel). This idea for a new kind of submersible came to him nearly thirty years before Beebe's bathy*sphere* dive, and more than a half-century before his own bathyscaphe

Trieste was actually to touch the lowest point on earth. Jacques Piccard, the son who was to pilot it there, was not even born.

While in college Piccard had read an account of a German oceanographic expedition made from a surface vessel, from which the men had tried to trawl for marine specimens. They had met with little success. Then and there he concluded that this was not the way to do it. Sitting on a mountain peak with his twin brother Jean, he had discussed his idea when they were twenty. To study underwater life, he argued, man would need a suitable free-floating balloon, lighter than water, with an attached cabin or gondola, watertight and able to withstand great pressure.

Many years had gone by since that day on the mountain. Now that he had used the pressurized cabin in the stratosphere, he was ready to get back to his original plan for it. He knew that three-quarters of the earth's surface is water. He also knew that 60.8 percent of that surface is *more than a mile underwater*. Here was a vast unexplored "laboratory" to challenge a scientist. If this area could be opened to man, the course of the future would inevitably be affected.

Soon after his successful stratospheric flight Auguste Piccard was given a reception by Belgium's King Leopold, son of King Albert (the man who had made the flight possible by allocating funds from his country's National Research Funds). Leopold found himself immediately drawn to the gentle, unassuming professor with the unexpected sense of humor. He took him aside and questioned him about his future plans. Piccard replied that he wanted to build a vessel able to take him to the floor of the deepest place in the ocean.

Leopold's interest was immediate. Piccard's recent stratospheric achievement merited respect, and Leopold's attention had recently been focused on the underseas by William Beebe's safe voyage to depths from which no man had hitherto returned alive.

Beebe's vessel, called a bathysphere, was intended primarily for observation purposes, just as Piccard's was to be. It was a round steel ball with fused quartz windows, attached to a surface ship by cable. It was lowered into the sea by winches, and the cable was "played out" from the ship. In this respect it was like a tethered balloon. Weight did not have to be considered, since Beebe's craft did not have to rise from the depths unassisted. It could be built of steel strong enough to resist the sea's pressure. Since it would be hauled up, it did not need to throw out ballast to rise. It would dangle in the water several thousand feet below the surface, providing an enclosed, on-the-scene site for its occupants.

Leopold, naturally enough, wanted to know why Beebe's bathysphere wasn't the answer to the study of the great depths. What need was there for Auguste Piccard's proposed bathyscaphe? Critics would be sure to say that Piccard was trying to "horn in" on the act for personal glory. They would accuse him of trying to minimize the feat of the man who had preceded him. Leopold questioned him at length on these points.

Piccard was loud in his praise of Beebe. Throughout his life he never ceased praising him for making the middle depths available for man's study . . . the area where the greatest variety of sea life exists. He gave Beebe and Barton full credit for being first to go underwater fully protected from external pressure. He himself had been first to do the same thing in the stratosphere. He had, he assured the King, sound reasons for wishing to build his own kind of submersible: he had detected a flaw in Beebe's. Its very lifeline, the cable from which it was suspended, was a source of danger.

The longer the cable, the greater its weight. The greater its weight, the greater its risk of breaking. Too, the rise and fall, pitch and toss of the surface ship was transmitted by the cable to the men hitched to it below, tossing them around uncomfortably and preventing any motionless observation of sea creatures. This constant motion increased the risk of a break which would catapult the men to the unreachable bottom where, buried alive, they would meet slow death in their steel casket. Then, there was the disadvantage that the bathysphere could not be allowed to touch bottom, which was the very place where Piccard intended to go! (Beebe was afraid that his vessel would get mired in the thick sediment of the ocean's floor. In any case, if his ship were resting on the bottom, the motion of the surface ship transmitted to it by the cable would be intensified.)

Certainly it was logical for the King to feel that Piccard's proposed craft, which had to be ballasted to go up and down freely, able to rise up against tons of resisting sea water, offered infinitely greater risk to its pilot than one which was suspended from a cable. Piccard didn't think so. The miracle is that he was able to convince King Leopold that his revolutionary idea was both plausible and practical.

Piccard told the King that he wanted to invent and construct a sort of depth dirigible able to move around freely on the bottom of the sea. His vessel would serve as a submerged laboratory for scientific observations, from which men could study and "mine" the infinite products of the ocean. He intended, he said, to make a journey in his craft "a perfectly safe venture for a family man." He was convinced that Beebe's craft did not offer such safety, and would not care, he said, to venture in it himself.

Auguste Piccard knew that his construction problems would be incomparably greater than Beebe's, but he never dreamed of the infinite number of them he would be required to overcome. He was not going to be hauled up from the depths, he must be able to rise unaided. He must invent an infallible way of doing it, against the pressure of all those tons of water. He would need to illuminate the inside of his cabin and the area around it for the total blackness of the abyssal depths. He must pass instruments through the cabin walls without weakening them. The simplest error in calculation would bring death to the pilots. No one would return from the depths to tell about it. He was prepared to spend years, testing every piece of material that went into his vessel. As problems developed, he expected to make the inventions necessary to solve them. He would learn as he went along. He could not rely on precedents, for there were none. He was proposing to do something which had never been done before. He would need to build many successive models, the first one intended for lesser depths, as he progressed toward his ultimate goal. When he reached that goal *he would go down himself.*

Surely it never crossed his mind that so many years would elapse, so many models would be needed along the way, that his ten-year-old son Jacques would grow to manhood, become his partner, and eventually pilot the Ultimate Dive, to the deepest place on earth.

Such an eventuality never occurred to Madame Piccard either. Time, she felt, was going to be working on her side. For a good many years her husband would be harmlessly occupied building scale models of his new idea. Most men liked to tinker, and this was good. She could look after her dear man, and minister to his health. She thought of him as safely grounded for the foreseeable future, happily engrossed with his queer new hobby.

Piccard's plan, to proceed step by step on his "new" project, is the natural course followed in developing all major new inventions. The first airplane, the first automobiles, were primitive compared to those of today. He did not reckon on the fact that the public, which had seen his stratospheric flights achieve their goal so quickly, would again expect an immediate miracle from him. There was a big difference this time. When he had undertaken the construction of his stratospheric balloon he had inherited the accumulated knowledge of 150 years of ballooning. He had adapted an existing balloon to new uses by pressurizing its cabin. Now he was proposing to start from scratch and create something altogether new.

Submarines would offer him no help. They had been in use for many years, but their cruising depth even today is limited to around 600 feet. In the 1930s, about 250 feet was their diving limit. The disasters to several submarines, including the

Thresher and *Scorpion*, are believed to have resulted from mechanical failures which dropped them to depths where pressure crushed their light steel hulls. This is called "implosion" — inward crushing from an outside force.

Why the simple logic of Piccard's procedure was so difficult to grasp is hard to understand today, when we have seen man reach for the moon in many successive stages. Haste would have provided a recipe for failure.

If Piccard could have foreseen the jeers he was to meet along the way, it would have made no difference to the orderly stages of his experiment. He was determined to remain a live husband, father and scientist, and not to become a dead adventurer. His thinking was not too different from that of Louis XVI, 150 years earlier. On the very first balloon flight the King had insisted on using animals. He had refused to risk the lives of human beings. Piccard expected to make the first *manned* descent himself. Before then he determined to send his vessel down empty, controlled by some sort of mechanism that would submerge and return it. In this way he would prove that it could make the round trip safely. Then, and only then, would he venture to take it down himself.

To do this would require vast sums of money, and the world was in the midst of the Great Depression! King Leopold turned him once again toward Belgium's Foundation for Scientific Research. Piccard was going to apply for funds for his second venture to the same source that had provided them for his first. He was not Belgian, he was Swiss. What were his chances?

Piccard referred to Belgium as his second country. For many years he had taught physics at the University of Brussels and had made his home there. Four of his five children had been born in Brussels. Yet it was hard for him to feel confidence that Belgium would again grant him the kind of financial help he needed so desperately.

It took a bit longer, even with the King's endorsement, but eventually the Belgian Foundation gave him a second grant. Its members reasoned that here was a man whose record showed that he could achieve the seemingly impossible. The newspapers had dubbed him "Columbus of the Atmosphere," and Belgium's *FNSR I* had received world acclaim. If Piccard was prepared to aim for the abyssal depths in a different kind of balloon, the Foundation would provide *FNSR II* for the journey.

With $25,000 at his disposal, Piccard set to work. A testing laboratory specializing in problems of high pressure was set up at the University of Brussels in 1937. Dozens of scale models were built and tested. In a preliminary trial one of them was subjected, in special tanks, to pressures which equaled the weight of a *ten-mile column of water*.

Piccard's first problem had been to make his vessel go down. This was his easiest. He had devised a float which corresponded to the envelope of a balloon, and he attached his watertight pressurized cabin to it. He planned to carry enough ballast, in the form of iron pellets, to force his ship down. To rise, he would get rid of the ballast. Then the buoyant float, filled with a substance lighter than water, would rise to the surface. Unfortunately this substance, gasoline, has greater compressibility than water. This meant that its lifting power would *lessen* as the craft went down. The bathyscaphe would become heavier and heavier as it descended. Theory and repeated tests had established this.

Then and there Piccard saw that ballast would play a more vital role in his bathyscaphe than it had in his stratospheric balloon. A balloonist who has used up all his ballast can rise no higher. He can let off his gas and come down again, even if he must brave a hard landing. When Piccard and Kipfer had broken their gas-release valve they had still managed to come down safely. The air in their balloon had *forced* them down by growing heavier as it cooled. There was no such natural force operating on behalf of the bathyscaphe pilot. Only by jettisoning ballast could he force himself *up*, in a vessel growing heavier as he descended. His ballast was all-important . . . his only means of lightening his craft. This ballast was attached to the outside of the cabin, and the pilot inside its walls had to be able to dump it.

Various means were tried. First, Piccard thought of a rod that shoved out the ballast. But tests showed that this way was unsure, in the increasing pressure of descent. Free movement of the shaft couldn't be guaranteed. The possibility of breakage, or of jamming, was ever present. Piccard abandoned the idea and turned toward an electrical solution of the problem.

His assistants threw up their hands in terror. Electricity had an attendant danger of short circuit. Who wanted to place his life in the constant jeopardy of a possible power failure? But Auguste Piccard decided to turn that risk to his advantage.

From it he would achieve a *guarantee* of safety. The ballast would be retained against the ship by electrical current. To dump it, the current would be switched *off*. Any kind of electrical failure would automatically drop the ballast and the ship would rise. The dive would be halted, but the pilot would be carried back to the surface. Auguste Piccard referred to this idea as his "fail-safe." Jacques Piccard called it his father's way of "falling up."

Piccard planned to carry three different sizes of iron pellets for ballast, in three different containers on the ship's exterior. Each container had its own switch, enabling it to be unloaded separately, thus allowing the pilot to control his rate of rise. Even the storage batteries that provided the power were suspended to the ship's outside. They were held to the casing of the electromagnets by electricity. In a desperate crisis these batteries too could be dropped. They served a double purpose — as a source of power and as additional emergency ballast. This precaution of making parts of his vessel releasable in a crisis was a major innovation pioneered by Piccard. It is regarded by today's boat designers and oceanographers as a major contribution to undersea safety. The world's smallest submarine, the twenty-three foot *Alvin*, invented by Alyn Vine, and constructed in 1964 for scientific research and United States naval defense, has similar features directly borrowed from Piccard's bathyscaphe. Piccard also had to figure out how much ballast to carry on his ship. Too little would be fatal, too much would add needlessly to the huge construction costs by requiring a larger float to offset the ballast's weight.

One by one he faced his problems and overcame them. He must have thought of the legendary Hydra, who grew two new heads each time one was lopped off. He achieved a way to make his craft go up and down, and to move about on the bottom powered by two electrically driven propellers. He even found a way to halt his vessel in mid-rise or mid-descent, and to keep it nearly stable in this suspended state, so that its occupants could make observations of nature at close hand, without frightening off the timid creatures of the deep. He developed and tested Plexiglas portholes so safe from both leakage and implosion that their copies are universally used in deep-sea vessels today.

This need to furnish a wide view of the submarine world to the bathyscaphe's occupants provided Auguste Piccard with a major problem. In his many experiments along the way to perfecting his windows, he had even tried using small peepholes made from the cones of diamonds. A diamond, the hardest known substance, can only be cut by another diamond. Yet at highest pressure, even these diamonds cracked. Most persons would have concluded that it was useless for man to strive for the great depths. What purpose would it serve to get there without being able to look out? This voyage was not supposed to be a feat of derring-do, nor was its purpose to establish a new depth record. Piccard was scornful of scientists who had what he termed "record psychosis." His journeys were to be undertaken to make scientific observations. Piccard made numerous experiments with many different materials before he achieved his safe porthole. Inside the cabin it encountered normal atmospheric pressure at all depths. Outside, in the great depths, it resisted pressure equaling the force of more than five hundred tons per square inch.

It was only after repeated failures with his portholes that Auguste Piccard's attention had been called to a substance new to the market called Plexiglas. This substance, in wide use today, is perfectly transparent and not nearly so hard as glass. It has a certain amount of elasticity, and if parts of it are overloaded it bends a bit and passes the excess load to adjacent parts, thus distributing the stresses uniformly throughout the entire surface. By contrast, glass, which lacks elasticity, yields to overload by cracking or shattering. Piccard made his windows cone-shaped, with the small aperture within the cabin at normal pressure. Outside in the vast pressures of the deep the cone widened like a V, increasing the visual field and offering a greater area for the distribution of stress. Piccard concluded that these windows, which he called "the finest feature of the bathyscaphe," could withstand pressure corresponding to 18.6 miles of depth, had such a depth existed. He has stated that never once during any of his dives did he worry for one instant about the possibility that his Plexiglas windows would crack. Had they done so, death to the bathyscaphe's occupants would of course have resulted almost immediately.

But it would be pointless to create one perfect part if another were to fail. The cabin too must resist *implosion*, which is inward crushing from an outside force, as contrasted to *explosion* where an object is blown apart by an internal force. Professor Piccard has stated that the problem posed by his cabin would have been "relatively easy" if he had

The top half of the bathyscaphe is put through radium X-ray tests to detect any impurities in the steel.

been able to build cabin walls of uniform thickness. That would have subjected them to uniform pressure. He was not able to do this. He had to cut holes in his cabin walls . . . for his portholes, for wires and tubes and hatch. The thickness of the walls around the holes had to be increased, and he had to make new calculations for these reinforced areas and the differing degrees of stress that they would encounter.

In test after test he placed exact scale models in tanks where pressure was increased progressively. He duplicated conditions that would exist in descent in the sea. He insisted on a "factor of safety." The models had to be able to withstand *more* pressure in his test tank than they would encounter in the ocean.

Relentlessly the exacting work went on. Two steps forward, one step backward. Trial and error, trial and error, the formula for success that his father had drilled into him in childhood. He must find a solution for any catastrophe or emergency that he could imagine. He had had one experience, in the stratosphere, of being beset by the unexpected and of having survived by sheer ingenuity, but deep under the surface of the alien sea there could be no makeshift measures. He would stake his own life on the judgments that he made in building his craft. He was unaware of it then, but his only son would do the same thing.

The years went by. The hands of time were moving relentlessly onward, and Piccard was fifty-five years old. There was no time to rest. But he had been lucky in finding an able young assistant, Jean Guillissen, who understood his ideas and was quick to execute them efficiently. They worked together smoothly. Construction on *FNSR II* was actually beginning. His boyhood dream was taking shape at last, coming into existence before his very eyes . . . Soon, very soon, he would be able to test his bathyscaphe in person, by taking it down to the great depths.

But it was 1939, and the world too was balanced on the brink of an abyss. At the very moment when Auguste Piccard's dream was within his grasp, Adolf Hitler tried to effect his own dream, and World War II broke out. . . .

AUGUSTE PICCARD RESUMED his teaching and went back to making experiments in various laboratories for the duration of the war. There was nothing else that he could do. Manpower and materials were at a premium. As a sensitive human being, Piccard was sickened by "man's inhumanity to man" and by the waste of war. As a scientist he abhorred the ensuing vacuum, and wondered if the day would ever come when he could resume his work for the advancement of knowledge for peaceful ends. The clock had become his enemy. . . .

Six years crawled by and it was 1945. A hush of devastation hung like a cloud over much of Europe, but the guns were silent at last. Now there was peace, with all its attendant problems. Auguste Piccard was over sixty. His young assistant had been killed by the Gestapo. The Belgian franc had been devalued by an inflation so severe that the purchasing power of the remnants of his grant was crippled. He had devoted twelve years to his bathyscaphe and hadn't completed one yet. Wasn't it time to quit, and to hand over his plans to someone else?

This idea never occurred to him. Without hesitation he went back to the Belgian Foundation. Its members had seen what he could accomplish. Surely they would make it possible for him to pick up where he had left off. A six-year delay was only a grain in the sands of Time. It should be viewed as one more of the many obstacles that persistence had overcome.

He was right. The Foundation was eager to help him, anxious to reap the results of all the expenditures of the past . . . but now money was its problem too. It was as scarce as the materials needed for the bathyscaphe's construction. Auguste Piccard, the man who hated shortcuts, was going to be faced with a hard fact — a vastly lessened budget which would force him to eliminate or modify many special features of his craft.

Equally hard for him to accept was the Foundation's decree that this time he must resume his undertaking with a Belgian as a full partner. Max Cosyns, a Belgian whom Piccard had selected as his assistant to replace his former one, was elevated to the post. He would share equally in the supervision of the project.

This was a bitter blow. Piccard could well understand the reasons for the Foundation's demand. For the third time, a Belgian organization was underwriting the costs of a Swiss venture. Now it was bowing to pressure from its members to share in the accomplishment. Piccard did not mind dividing the honors. That aspect had never been important to him. He feared the inherent dangers of a plan which destroyed his absolute authority to make decisions.

Handicapped by lack of funds, it took three more years to complete an economy version of his original concept. Only one fact dulled the edges of his sorrow over the loss of time. His son Jacques was now twenty-six years old, and he would accompany the expedition on the first deep-dive tests at Dakar, off the southern coast of Africa. There had not even been enough money to make the preliminary tests in home waters that Auguste Piccard had urged. An inexperienced crew would gamble on success in unknown waters. Jacques Piccard, describing the vessel that would take the gamble, said in his book: "Every nut and bolt is expected to do the work of two."

Two ways of getting the *FNSR II* to the site of the dives had been considered. It could be loaded on a large cargo ship and taken there. Upon arrival the pilots could climb into the watertight cabin from the cargo ship's hold. Once the bathyscaphe's hatch had been closed it could be lifted by crane and deposited on the sea, ready to begin its dive. But the combined weight of the bathyscaphe and of the gasoline that filled its float was enormous. No cargo ship possessing adequate hoisting equipment was available.

The men considered a second way around the problem. It might be possible to tow the bathyscaphe and its gasoline-filled float to the diving place. This would be best. But it would require a float strong enough to withstand the rigors to which towing would subject it in heavy seas. Expense ruled out constructing such a float. Thus a decision was forced on Piccard. The submarine would be launched with an empty float. The men would enter the cabin and be sealed in. Then the gasoline would be pumped in. When the dive was over the float would need to be pumped dry before the men could come out of the cabin. It was a dangerous and awkward procedure and Piccard wasn't happy about it, but lack of money left him no choice.

Now began the search for a suitable ship, and once again the Belgian government stepped in. Construction was started on *Scaldis*, a 3500-ton steam-powered cargo ship. Its main hold, which would stow the *FNSR II*, would also house a workshop to be used en route. All other holds would carry freight. *Scaldis* would then bring back native produce on scheduled stops on the return trip. This would help defray costs, when every penny counted. It also put a time limit on the dives. They would have to take place in the brief time that the *Scaldis* was at Piccard's disposal.

Men have always spoken of their ships in the feminine gender. Some attribute it to the love they feel for them, and the admiration for their grace and beauty. Others, less kind, say it is because ships are temperamental and require careful handling. In any case, superstitions about ships are many. No crew would sail with a cross-eyed cook. The champagne bottle must break as it strikes the ship's bow at launching time, else disaster is prophesied.

No such ill omens marred the launching of the

Scaldis for its shakedown cruise to the Baltic, but the voyage was not a happy one. There was engine trouble. The ship struck a shoal and narrowly avoided shipwreck. A defective valve caused trouble, and a damaged steampipe. All of these things were corrected in transit. Still, the fifty members of Piccard's crew muttered: No good would come of the trip. The *Scaldis* was an unlucky ship!

Scarcity of money had figured in the choice of Dakar, off the coast of South Africa, as the site for the dives. It was not too far from Antwerp, the Belgian port of departure. Storms were infrequent in the area. Most important of all, its waters offered depths of 3.75 miles. On the final dive of the expedition Piccard intended to make a manned descent to 2.5 miles. To put into effect his "factor of safety," he would send the bathyscaphe down 50 percent farther, to the 3.75-mile depth. It would be taken there by a robot pilot.

On September 15, 1948, *Scaldis* weighed anchor for the journey. Crowds of reporters and spectators had gathered to wave the expedition off. Auguste Piccard was the lion of the hour. He was accompanied by his son Jacques, his associate Max Cosyns and Mrs. Cosyns, a Frenchman (Professor

Monod), two young Belgian biologists, an oceanographer, a physician, a photographer and a publicity officer provided by the Belgian government.
Jacques Piccard, Max Cosyns, the biologists and
the oceanographer expected to take turns accompanying Auguste Piccard to the bottom in successive and progressively deeper dives. Each manned
dive would be preceded by an unmanned test dive
to greater depths.

Science knows few frontiers. When an advance
in man's knowledge is at stake, nationalism is put
aside. Almost all countries share in the excitement
and are eager to cooperate. As the *Scaldis* steamed
into Dakar it was met by a French naval vessel
fitted out for oceanographic research. The *Elie
Monnier* was a floating base for the famous French
scuba diver Jacques Cousteau. He was aboard,
heading an enthusiastic welcoming committee. All
of the ship's facilities were put at Piccard's disposal. The generous help of the French engineers
and officers was welcomed, for there were still
many verifications which Auguste Piccard needed
to make. The Portuguese Navy also cooperated
by allowing the French naval vessel to enter its
territorial waters off the nearby Cape Verde
Islands, the area selected for the dives. This per-

mission enabled the *Elie Monnier*'s echo sounders to pinpoint the most favorable spot for the descent.

There had been a major change in plans. Auguste Piccard and Max Cosyns had decided to go down on the first dive, after all. It would be a short one, fourteen fathoms (seventy-four feet). Their purpose was to check out the ship's equipment before sending the valuable bathyscaphe to the great depths. They had rigged the *FNSR II* with a time switch designed to set off the unballasting which would bring it back to the surface. There was also a mechanism designed to unballast the ship and bring it up in case of water leakage in the cabin. The men were going down to observe the automatic performance in what they hoped could be a "hands off" ride.

On the afternoon of October 26, all preparations were completed. At this moment Max Cosyns decided not to go. He had been ill, and this may have influenced his decision. At any rate he chose to view the operation from the deck of the *Scaldis*. As all of the observers were eager to take his place in the first dive of them all, Professor Piccard decided to play fair and not favor his son Jacques. Lots were drawn and the coveted honor fell to Professor Monod. The others would have to wait their turn in subsequent dives.

It was a memorable moment for Auguste Piccard. He and his companion went to the hold of the *Scaldis* and entered *FNSR*'s cabin by its manhole. The lid was bolted down behind them and they were more completely cut off from the world than today's astronauts-in-orbit, as the telephone was not yet in commission. The big crane swung them smoothly upward, then lowered them into the sea. Now the portholes were submerged and a ghostly blue light flooded the cabin. The men were calm enough to observe its beauty and to comment on it. Next came the resonant echo of gasoline cascading into the bathyscaphe's float. The process required a seemingly endless time and the men staved off impatience by playing chess. At last the slow descent began. Then *FNSR II* grounded easily without shock or jar on the bottom fourteen fathoms below sea level. Its occupants looked out on an empty underwater plain ridged into scalloped furrows by the action of the sea.

Here was a chance to increase their knowledge. Auguste Piccard, still interested in the study of cosmic rays that had led him into the stratosphere, had installed instruments to measure their density underwater. He found that even at this limited depth, cosmic radiation had been affected. It had been diminished by the water's absorption.

Now the time switch went into action, the unballasting took place without a hitch, and at ten o'clock at night the bathyscaphe broke the smooth surface of the sea. Piccard and Monod had been inside the cabin for seven hours and were eager to come out, but a long wait was ahead of them. There was gasoline to be drained out of the float, and the bathyscaphe must be lifted back to the hold of the *Scaldis* by crane. Five more hours dragged by and it was three o'clock in the morning. The delay was tedious and uncomfortable for the men in their cramped quarters, but Auguste Piccard only shrugged his shoulders and reopened the chess board. What were twelve hours at sea level to a man who had once spent seventeen hours in an airtight cabin in the stratosphere? The first bathyscaphe dive had been successful and that was all that mattered.

Now the *Scaldis* headed out to another island in the Cape Verde group, seeking the 770-fathom depth that Piccard wanted for the first unmanned descent. His faith in his automatic pilot was secure, and Piccard was willing to risk his vessel to it.

But he had dreamed up one final precaution and he was to regret it. He had begun to worry about the French vessel's echo finder, and its ability to reckon the sea's depth exactly. Piccard wanted no hard and injurious landing for his craft if the bottom were nearer than had been indicated. He installed a long antenna on the bottom of the bathyscaphe. On contact with the ocean floor it would trigger the mechanism that released the ballast. But during the launching, at the exact moment when *FNSR II* crossed the rail of the *Scaldis*, a rope swung out from the mother ship. It touched the end of the antenna. Everyone had a chance to see how well the antenna functioned, when many tons of ballast cascaded into the sea, while the observers stood helplessly by!

This caused a serious loss of time. It took four days to get ready for another try. The depth gauge was set for 770 fathoms. The time switch was set to its maximum . . . twelve hours. Then began the long procedure for takeoff. Several hours went by. Suddenly the men realized that the *Scaldis* had drifted in the current, and new depth soundings had showed only 495 fathoms beneath her. This forced them to tow the bathyscaphe, which was now in the water, to a new location. The towing line broke and had to be repaired. The observers began to grow frantic at the losing race with the time clock. It was impossible to reset it, for it was within *FNSR II*'s cabin, which was now underwater.

With only forty minutes left before automatic unballasting, the bathyscaphe went down at last, leaving its anxious observers behind. Some feared that they would never see it again, and said so. Piccard had no worries on this score. What he feared was that time would run out before *FNRS II* reached the bottom. He did not know its exact rate of descent, but it seemed improbable that it could reach the desired depth. After its return they would know. The recording depth gauge would tell them exactly how far down the bathyscaphe had traveled.

Piccard took up his vigil, telescope in hand. He scanned the sea, dotted with observation launches and small boats. He did mental calculations. Forty minutes to descend, and then the time needed for the rise . . . plenty of time to go below for a cup of tea, but he could not bring himself to leave his post. He was so sure that the *FNSR II* would return that he began thinking about tomorrow's manned dive to the depth it had achieved. That would be the safe way. Increasingly deep dives, robot-piloted, and then matching dives in which the observers would take turns accompanying him. There would be time for half a dozen dives before the *Scaldis* had to leave for home. A new depth record would no doubt be set.

Once again he made a wide arc, sweeping the sea with his telescope. He picked up a brilliant orange spot in the distance, and he looked at his watch. *Twenty-nine minutes!* He couldn't dare think that the bathyscaphe had made the round trip, over a mile and a half, in that short time! Something must have gone wrong. Perhaps the cabin had sprung a leak, setting off the automatic unballasting! The answer was locked inside the cabin. The observers must wait until it could be opened.

FNSR II was brought alongside the *Scaldis* and everyone clustered around, while all the surrounding boats tooted their horns. Suddenly the wind rose and the submarine was swept with great waves that bumped it dangerously against the mother ship. The crew climbed aboard the bathyscaphe and tried to attach the big hose to drain off the gasoline. They couldn't manage it in the rough seas that swept clear across the bathyscaphe. Again and again they tried, and were almost washed overboard. A shark circled the vessel, its ominous black fin clearly visible above the frothy water. . . . Tow lines were hastily rigged, as the vessel couldn't be lifted back aboard the *Scaldis* because of its heavy load of gasoline.

Slowly the *Scaldis*, towing the valuable craft, moved toward a sheltering bay, while the bathyscaphe's metal plates groaned in anguish at the punishment of the angry sea. *FNSR II* had not been built for this sort of travel. It was intended for the eternal calm of the great depths. Night fell, and as Auguste Piccard looked back at the now-dim outlines of the bathyscaphe, it seemed to him that she was beginning to sink. He couldn't be sure, but he couldn't risk it. All that money, and a span of seventeen years! He made a quick decision and a hard one. The gasoline must be dumped into the sea. Carbon dioxide, inserted through a narrow tube, must replace it in the float, to keep out heavier sea water.

He gave the order with a sinking heart. The loss of the gasoline would mean the end of the whole expedition. No further dives could take place, manned or unmanned. But even that was a small price to pay for the safety of the bathyscaphe!

The *Scaldis* did not reach the quiet Bay of Santa Clara until dawn. The intervening hours had seemed endless to Auguste Piccard. What would the recording gauge show? Perhaps the whole costly venture had been a failure. He knew now what in his heart he had always known . . . that his next dives must be made in a bathyscaphe built to withstand towing in rough seas. The present un-

The *FNRS II*, showing signs of water pressure, is propped up on a Dakar dock next to the *Scaldis*.
UPI

wieldy launching methods had been a makeshift, dictated by lack of money. His tall son Jacques, denied his chance to dive, stood beside him, silently sharing his anxiety. Neither of them knew that for the next twelve years Jacques would captain every dive. They could not even feel sure that there would be any more dives. . . .

The bathyscaphe was lifted back aboard the *Scaldis* without incident, and trembling fingers opened its hatch. Then Auguste Piccard experienced one of the great moments of his life. The recording gauge showed that *FNSR II* had dived 759 fathoms, and returned to the surface. Admittedly there were a few drops of water in the cabin, caused by a loosened joint. The amount was too insignificant to have triggered off unballasting partway down, and a *human* pilot could easily have tightened the joint in descent. *If the dive had been manned it would have set a new depth record.* But that was hindsight. Foresight demanded that no gambles be taken with human lives. Piccard did not intend to alter that procedure.

Scaldis was now due in French Equatorial Africa to collect freight, and the twelve members of the expedition flew home. They landed back in Brussels to a very different kind of reception. They had left as lions, and they returned as lepers. The press pointed out that their only manned descent, to seventy-four feet, could easily have been duplicated by a scuba diver. Beebe's recent world record established in a dive in his captive bathysphere had not been seriously challenged. The fact that an empty *FNSR II* had made a safe round-trip dive to 4554 feet seemed to impress no one. Yet it had encountered and withstood exactly the same rigorous conditions of stress and pressure that it would have done with Piccard aboard. The newspapers dealt savagely with Auguste Piccard, suggesting that he had hoodwinked the public and misused the Belgian Foundation's funds.

Piccard was amazed. He was a scientist. He knew how many eons of time had gone into the creation of man. From the atom to the molecule to the single cell to the colonies of cells . . . then Nature had proceeded at her own unhurried pace to forms with specialized organs, until at last she had evolved the human brain. If she had required all this time it was surely not unreasonable to expect a short period of experimentation for a new human endeavor. He shrugged his shoulders in bewilderment. It was not important that he was personally discredited. *FNSR II* was no failure in his eyes.

All that he needed were the financial resources to perfect it. But who would provide them? This adverse publicity might well prove disastrous. Who would give him another chance?

part 2

5

AUGUSTE PICCARD HAD been right to worry about the adverse reaction of his sponsors, the Belgian Science Foundation. Seventeen years had gone by since he had carried their *FNSR I* into the stratosphere. That was ancient history to the new members and directors who made up the organization today. More vast sums of money would be required to modify the structure of a new bathyscaphe, and the Belgian group was no longer prepared to invest its funds in a Swiss venture whose outcome now seemed highly speculative. The Belgian Foundation signed an agreement with the French Navy and the French National Center of Scientific Research. The French Navy would take over the *FNSR II* and use its cabin as a nucleus for a new bathyscaphe, to be called *FNSR III*. The new vessel would belong to the Belgians until three deep dives had been made. Then ownership would be transferred to the French Navy. Auguste Piccard,

The *FNRS III* arrives in Paris.

who was neither a Frenchman nor a sailor, would
serve as the project's scientific adviser.

Piccard's help should have been invaluable. As
an experimental physicist as well as the inventor
of the bathyscaphe, he did make many useful suggestions. But he was hampered by lack of rank.
The French Navy had a complicated chain-of-
command, and endless red tape delayed progress
maddeningly. Ideas that he gave freely were given
a slight twist and dubbed "French inventions."
For the first time in all his long years of scientific

work he encountered professional jealousy. He was hampered at every turn and found his working conditions intolerable. All the way back to Galileo and Copernicus, scientists had known instinctively that creative minds must be free from the shackles of authority to pursue knowledge wherever they find it. Auguste Piccard was no exception.

Just when the clouds were darkest, everything changed. A group of industrialists from Trieste, Italy, invited Auguste Piccard to undertake the construction of a new bathyscaphe. He would serve as physicist-engineer-in-chief, with absolute authority in planning and construction.

It was like rolling back the clock to the early days when he had built his first bathyscaphe, in sole command of the undertaking. He informed the French Navy of his new plans and departed, leaving them all his instruments and the cabin of the *FNSR II*, which was to be used by them without adaptation. He was happier than he had been in years. He rejoiced to think that the simultaneous construction of *two* bathyscaphes would speed up the exploration of the great depths.

Now his son Jacques joined forces with him, and together they gave their full time to the construction of the new bathyscaphe *Trieste*. It was to be

UPI

Auguste Piccard watches as son Jacques emerges from an exact model of the cabin for the *Trieste*. This cabin, although essentially unchanged in principle, improved the safety and comfort of its pilots by allowing them to enter and exit at will.

built along the same principles as his *FNSR II*, but with some radical structural changes. . . .

The cabin remained unchanged, except that it was strengthened by being forged instead of cast. The general principle of a watertight cabin attached to a gasoline-filled float was retained. But this time the bathyscaphe was designed to be towed. The need for an accompanying hoist and crane had been eliminated. The *Trieste* would not have to be lifted perilously into the sea at the outset of each dive, and then taken out at its conclusion. The pilots would not need to enter it from the hold of the mother ship and then wait for hours in the cabin while gasoline was pumped into the float above them. They would not be trapped there, subject to all kinds of accident, once the gasoline was aboard. They could enter or leave the cabin at will, and in the open sea, through a shaft which ran through the float and into the cabin beneath it.

True, there was still a shortage of money, for the *Trieste* was being financed by private citizens, but many Swiss individuals and industrialists had added their substantial contributions. There was no money to throw around, and Auguste and Jacques Piccard were to regret the lack of an echo finder, although many safety features had been added. The construction features were the best the world offered. Quality materials were once again available. In the early postwar days they had been non-existent, and their lack had hampered the performance of *FNSR II*.

The *Trieste* was constructed in little more than a year. On the great day of its launching it flaunted

After 15 years of struggling, the *Trieste* is finally constructed completely to Auguste Piccard's satisfaction.

two flags, Italian and Swiss, an appropriate tribute to the faith and generosity of the two nations that had made it possible. Auguste Piccard's satisfaction with it was absolute. It had been such a long wait! He hadn't been young even back in 1937 when he had begun working on his first bathyscaphe. That was fifteen years ago, and here at last, except for a few frills, was the bathyscaphe of his dreams.

He considered himself greatly blessed. Besides

his loyal and patient wife he had four gentle daughters and a son with a strength of purpose to match his own. Jacques Piccard's total dedication to his father's project and his unswerving faith in its ultimate success had bolstered Auguste Piccard's courage during the years when his strength was dwindling. It was Jacques who had kept his spirits up all the long months when the ambiguous post that he held with *FNSR III* had frayed his nerves. If time ran out on him, Jacques would finish the job!

But this was no day to think about that. Auguste Piccard was still hale and hearty, and the first deep dives were about to begin.

part $\dfrac{2}{6}$

ON THE TWENTY-FIFTH of August, 1953, the *Trieste* began its long tow to Capri. Three shallow dives had been carried out as carefully as a dress rehearsal. Now they were about to begin a series of deep dives. Jacques Piccard and his father had become so certain of the safety and performance of their new bathyscaphe that they had decided to eliminate the unmanned tests. The two of them would go down together on the deep dives. They would assume the risks that they did not yet wish others to undertake.

Millions of persons have shared via television the excitement of the splash-downs of the astronauts. Somehow the tension is almost at its greatest then. A dangerous journey has been made, but to little purpose if the men can't make it back and emerge from their ship unscathed. No one can pinpoint the exact landing spot ahead of time, and the general area is ringed with vessels who form a veritable rescue cordon, ready to move fast if the need arises. Astronauts didn't yet exist that day at Capri, but similar arrangements were made for the "splash-up" of the *Trieste*. Ships were kept off two or three miles from the diving zone. The Italian corvette *Fenice* patrolled the area, with sixty journalists aboard.

The Piccards had selected a hollow 3630 feet deep off the southern side of Capri, as the diving site. There were deeper places farther off, but they would start here and increase the depth of each successive dive.

Even the elements are auspicious. The weather, which has been stormy, has grown calm and the two men climb aboard. The aging Professor Piccard, now sixty-nine, is a tall man, but he is dwarfed by the handsome young six-foot-seven-inch giant beside him. It is Jacques Piccard who is in command of the dive.

Flash bulbs pop and the reporters aboard the *Fenice* scribble furiously, trying to capture the scene on paper. There are none on hand who had witnessed Auguste Piccard's first stratospheric flight in 1931. At that time a newspaperman had said that if Auguste Piccard hadn't existed, a caricaturist would have had to invent him. Now time has frosted the shaggy mane and his thin old bones

The *Trieste*, off Capri, Italy, prepares to make the first series of deep dives as the Italian Navy Frigate, *Tenace*, stands by.

look brittle. Countless discouraging setbacks have furrowed his great brow. But his weak eyes are burning with purpose and excitement, and he stands erect. In old age Auguste Piccard is a fitting subject for portraiture.

The two men step into the cabin of the *Trieste*, close its door and receive the messages and information transmitted to them by telephone. Each time a directive is called down to them there is a double-check from the surface.

"Have you completed the assignment?"

"Are you both satisfied that it is executed properly?"

114

Nothing is left to chance or to the unlikely but undeniable possibility of nervously induced oversight.

From the surface the voice keeps them informed about what is happening, until the *Trieste* is fully submerged and the telephone is disconnected, leaving the father and son together in total isolation. The great moment has come, the one that, heartbreakingly, they had not had on *FNSR II*. The dive begins.

The anticlimax that follows is as swift as it is total. Ballast begins pouring out the front tank and the *Trieste* surfaces almost immediately. Is this going to be the shortest dive on record? Neither of the Piccards can endure the thought, especially as *FNSR III*, now completed, has just set a record in a manned dive to 1150 fathoms. They hold a hasty conference. Failure at the outset of the *Trieste* dives could cast a pall of gloom on the whole enterprise and shake the faith of their new sponsors. Repairs could take a week or more, while dismay mounted and confidence was undermined. Yet the trouble cannot be corrected underwater. What should they do?

It is Jacques Piccard who comes up with the dilemma's daring and ingenious solution. He suggests that they seal off the faulty tank and replace the weight of the lost ballast with the sacks of emergency supply aboard the *Fenice*.

Auguste Piccard examines the suggestion from every angle. If adopted it will mean that the dive can be resumed that very afternoon, and completed before nightfall. But is it safe to go down with a single working tank? His judgment must be dispassionate, unaffected by personal pride, for not only his life but his son's is at stake. Both men agree that the loss of the useful functioning of one tank adds no real risk to a dive of 550 fathoms. The undamaged tank contains enough ballast to bring them back from that depth. But their safety won't depend on the performance of the remaining tank. If worst comes to worst it is always possible to jettison the tank itself, and even the electromagnet valves.

Having made the decision, they carried out the plan without delay, and in the early afternoon the descent began again, smoothly and without difficulty. Afterwards Auguste Piccard was to be asked many times what he felt, at this moment that had been preceded by so many years of preparation. He always insisted that neither he nor his son experienced any fear for their physical safety.

What was there to frighten them? They were not going to be crushed. Hundreds of tests had proved that the *Trieste* could withstand the pressure of far greater depths than this one. They knew that they could rise at will, by cutting off the electricity that would release the ballast that was forcing them down. Then their vessel, lighter than the surrounding water, would be forced upward. Their only worry was that their dive might be cut short, and that some sort of electrical failure might force them up before they had reached the bottom toward which they were heading.

They were so relaxed that they made enjoyable observations as they descended. At 1500 feet down, in total darkness, they saw weirdly shaped luminous creatures. Now, as the pressure increased, the gasoline compressed and grew heavier, and their speed of descent increased. This frightened away the sea creatures, and the men were tempted to throw out small amounts of ballast to slow down the bathyscaphe. They could, if they wanted, even hold it in equilibrium, and then make zoological observations. They discussed the idea and concluded that the purpose of this particular dive was to establish *Trieste*'s ability to go down 3300 feet. The temptation must be resisted. They continued on and touched bottom so gently that they were not even aware of it.

Both men knew that sediment from above is constantly wafting down to the depths, providing additional food for creatures of the deep who, when they are not eating each other, exist on what they can extract from this rain of particles. In the upper layers, solar rays create chlorophyll in the algae and plant life found there, and small creatures eat these organic substances. As the water deepens, screening out the sunlight, plant life disappears and fish must catch what they can from the particles that drift down past them on the way to the bottom. Piccard had questioned oceanographers and been told that the sedimentary deposit on the sea floor deepened by about 1 millimeter, or 1/25 of an inch a year. Over the centuries it hardened, forming a base for the soft substance. He was told to expect, as a rule, an ooze approximately three feet deep. The *Trieste*, taking this into account, carried its ballast well up along its sides, so that its release would not be hindered. This particular dive, taking place off Capri, and distant from any river, led Auguste Piccard to expect to find a very slight deposit.

The bathyscaphe had come to a standstill and

the men exhaled in relief. They had made it to the bottom. Now they turned on the cabin lights, glanced at the porthole and experienced a deep shock. They were sunk in mud right up to its lower rim! That meant that the ooze must be well over four feet deep. None of *Trieste*'s exterior lights could pierce it, and their only illumination came from the lights inside the cabin.

Could they make the bathyscaphe rise out of the muck? They were like a ship that has run aground, but with the difference that they could not count on a rising tide to lift them. They must let off ballast and they could only do it from one tank. The other tank was still with them and in position, but it had been sealed off when it had lost its ballast.

For a moment Auguste Piccard must have experienced the same sensation that he had felt twenty-one years earlier when he and Paul Kipfer had been trapped in the stratosphere. But he and Jacques knew that they could, if need be, jettison the actual tanks. First they would let off ballast from the operating tank, hoping that this would lighten their load enough to lift them clear of the mud and its suction. They hoped not to have to scrap their tanks, but it was for such emergencies that Auguste Piccard had created his "fail-safes."

119

They threw the switch on the functioning tank and waited to see whether or not the *Trieste* would rise. They could not even be sure that the precious iron pellets of ballast were running out, able to make their way through the encompassing mud. It was the tensest moment of the dive.

For an endless minute nothing happened. Then the *Trieste* began to sway, like a creature trying to extricate itself from the tentacles of an octopus as it pulled itself up from the engulfing mud. They heard no sound, but the opaque mud at the porthole changed to cloudy water. They were rising! They rushed to the porthole and looked down, but the water, stirred up, hid the bottom from view. They were more than glad to bid the ocean's floor good-bye.

The speed of their ascent increased as they mounted and the gasoline expanded, and once again they were able to observe the phosphorescent creatures of the deep in their natural surroundings as they shot past. They were in total darkness. Then glimmers of light began to reach them, increasing and intensifying as they mounted. Not until they reached the surface did the cabin begin to rock very slightly. Now the sunlight, glancing off the waves of the sea's surface, was dazzling.

Small boats converged toward them, and the *Fenice* as well. Journalists swarmed around them, firing questions. Seals were broken off the depth indicators, providing instrumental proof that the *Trieste* had reached its goal. It had gone down over 550 fathoms. It had not yet equaled *FNSR III*'s most recent dive, but Auguste and Jacques Piccard were happy with the day's accomplishment. They were of one mind. They would continue to make haste slowly until the great day came when the *Trieste* would set its sights for the bottom of the world. . . .

The second dive followed in just a month, and this time Auguste and Jacques Piccard set a new depth record, 10,390 feet, just short of two miles. The dive itself was uneventful, but when they returned they were given the kind of reception usually reserved for admirals. Auguste Piccard, already known as the Columbus of the Atmosphere, now shared with his son Jacques the honorary title of Admiral of the Abyss.

The season was growing late, and it was time to put the *Trieste* in drydock for the winter. Jacques Piccard made one more dive, for a final check-out. It would be wise to go down and drop off both ballast tanks, to find out what would happen to the

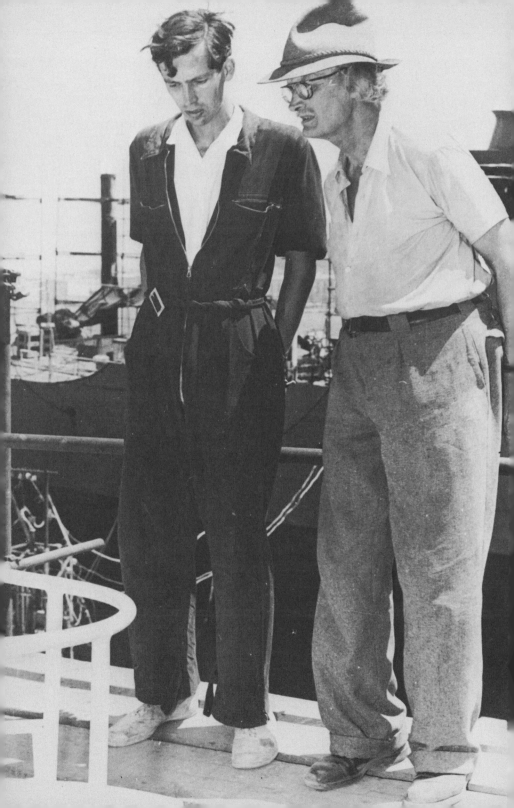

Trieste if he ever had to do so under emergency conditions. When he resumed his dives next year he intended to take oceanographers down with him, and he would not risk subjecting them to something that he had not previously experienced. He made his dive, dropped his tanks as planned, and was catapulted back at a rate of speed great enough to bend the flagstaff of the *Trieste*, but the ship suffered no other damage. The *Trieste* could withstand such a journey if need arose. That was all he wanted to know.

With the bathyscaphe tied up for the winter, Jacques Piccard now undertook his most delicate mission. He and his father had conferred, and both had agreed that the time had come for Auguste Piccard to become an observer rather than a participant in future dives. Jacques Piccard loved his father deeply, almost to the point of veneration. He had never known him to harbor a shabby thought. He had never known his courage to fail, in the face of ridicule or financial obstacles or physical danger. Now Jacques felt that the hazardous test dives in which they had both participated were over. Auguste Piccard had made them at nearly seventy, a time when most men have taken to the rocking chair. He had just set the newest depth record in

123

Auguste and Jacques Piccard discuss a problem aboard the *Trieste*.

the submersible that he had invented and spent a quarter of a century perfecting. But records had never been his goal, and he didn't feel old! Jacques knew that it was easy to postpone retirement. He racked his brain and came up with a convincing point. His father should let his place in the *Trieste* be taken by marine scientists who, one at a time, were eager to be given a direct view of the vast realm of the great depths. Newspapermen, anxious to make headlines, had depicted the *Trieste* as a vehicle for adventurers and death-defying show-offs. Its serious purpose, as a vessel designed to serve science by increasing man's knowledge of the abyssal realm, had been overlooked. Now, properly tested, it was ready to fulfill the mission for which it had been built. There were hundreds of questions waiting to be answered. How did fish resist the pressure of the great depths which could crush the steel hulls of submarines? How did they communicate with each other? How did they see in total darkness? Why were some of them gaily colored, when their color served no apparent purpose if it could not be seen? What was the geological age of some of the great submarine canyons on the bottom of the sea? How old was the floor of the deep ocean which had never been drained of its covering miles of water? Where was the source of some of the great undersea rivers that stream in varying directions, one above another in the depths? Only the experts could find the answers, and Auguste Piccard had blazed the way. He had made it possible for them to go down to the abyss and make firsthand observations, by providing a

Auguste Piccard sits on a wooden plank watching workmen load gasoline onto the *Trieste*. At the age of nearly 70 he was finally to give up diving and leave future descents to his son, Jacques.

UPI

vessel capable of besting the obstacles that had barred the way. He had accomplished his mission. Jacques, in turn, would accomplish his by piloting them there.

Logic, lovingly applied, hastened the day. After one farewell descent in 1954, Jacques's father surfaced for good. Auguste Piccard had made his last dive!

conclusion

THE REST OF the story belongs to Jacques Piccard. On January 23, 1960, he and Lieutenant Donald Walsh, U.S.N., penetrated to the lowest depth of Inner Space, and landed the *Trieste* on the very bottom of the world, almost seven miles straight down. . . .

It didn't happen overnight. Six more years, in which triumphs alternated with disappointments, were needed. When, on the eve of the great dive, someone pointed out to Jacques Piccard that he had labored ten years for this day, he only shrugged. It had been over fifty years since his father had first conceived the idea of an underwater balloon, and almost thirty since he began work on his first one. What was a decade, compared to half a century?

For a whole year after he and Auguste Piccard, holding a new depth record by their dive off Capri, had put the *Trieste* in drydock, the bathyscaphe remained tied up there. No money could be found to launch a new series of dives. It was private assistance from generous individuals that had made the *Trieste* possible, and except for the help of the Italian Navy, no government was bearing any part of the burden. Yet all the while the world was growing increasingly mindful of the imperative need to develop the new science of oceanography. Jacques Piccard once stated solemnly that the cost of the iron pellets used in ballasting the bathyscaphe was "25 cents for each yard of descent." He had grown so used to counting pennies that it was routine for him to scrounge for paltry sums entirely disproportionate to the value of the undertaking.

He and his father had spent most of that frustrating year of 1955 searching for additional funds. They had been turned down by science foundations in Washington when they had sought help for a series of dives off the great trench near Puerto Rico, even though they had offered to collaborate with American oceanographers. Although the *Trieste* was drydocked only a few short miles from Naples, headquarters for the U. S. Navy's 6th Fleet, only one officer had bothered to visit the *Trieste*. Yet there was only one other bathyscaphe in the world, *FNSR III*, which was now owned by the French Navy.

By 1956 Jacques Piccard had garnered a slim

fund from Swiss and Italian groups, and with a geologist from the University of Milan he made six dives, descending to over 12,000 feet and acquiring valuable scientific data.

His luck hadn't turned until 1956 when fate stepped in, in the person of Robert S. Dietz, who was later to become Jacques Piccard's collaborator in writing *Seven Miles Down*. Dietz, an American oceanographer attached to the London branch of the U. S. Office of Naval Research, met Jacques Piccard there at a lecture, and asked to be taken to view the *Trieste*. One visit was enough. Jacques Piccard had found what he needed most, an advocate to help him plead his cause in Washington. For a year the ONR sponsored a whole new series of diving tests in *Trieste* in the Mediterranean. Satisfied on every count at last, it bought the *Trieste* in 1958.

To Jacques Piccard, it was like selling a part of himself, but he had no choice. Then, when the contract was drawn but not yet signed, Russia launched her Sputnik into orbit. Jacques Piccard found the fortitude to keep his thoughts to himself as he saw millions of dollars immediately made available to space agencies for the race to the moon! When, on the eve of the Great Dive, he stood

Wide World Photos

The *Trieste* sets out for its record dive of 37,800 feet to the ocean bottom of the Mariannas Trench.

poised off Guam for his assault on the Challenger Deep, it was not bitterness that he felt, but joy. The day had been more than half a century in the making, but it had come at last. It was a testimonial to the invincibility of the human spirit. . . .

Jacques Piccard hadn't slept much that night before the final dive. Lying in his bunk on the U.S.S. *Wandank,* he had listened to the rising wind and heard the rattle of the iron pellets cascading into the ballast tanks of the *Trieste.* There was also the constant noise of the TNT explosions, for the team of scientists aboard the destroyer escort was seeking to locate the deepest hole in the Deepest Hole! It took *eight hundred* detonations, each interpreted on the echo sounder, to satisfy them that they had succeeded.

As he and Lieutenant Walsh climbed aboard a *Trieste* wallowing in heavy seas the next day, Jacques Piccard was doing mental arithmetic. Ballast had to be conserved, doled out with accuracy and precision on this long journey, for it would be vitally important to control their rate of descent and to maintain the buoyancy of the ship. He had learned to transmute the *weight* of the ballast into terms of *time*. If he disposed of it at a rate of twenty-five pounds per second, there would be enough ballast for almost exactly twenty-four hours of continuous travel. That should be more than ample for the round trip. The men made a final inspection of their equipment, Jacques Piccard, as pilot of the voyage, gave the signal, and the historic dive began.

They moved steadily downward. At 340 feet they encountered the first of a series of thermal barriers which halted descent and even bounced them about a bit. This was the result of the density of the cold water at that depth, and its resistance to the ship's penetration. They pushed past this opposing force and continued downward on their long journey to the bottom of the world. Adding inevitably to the tension was the knowledge garnered from arduously prepared charts that the great cleft into which they were heading was only a mile wide. It would be entirely possible to collide with the trench's wall! Speed of descent must be reduced as they neared the bottom, for the sake of safety.

Now they entered the world of the abyssal depths, and the inside of the *Trieste*'s cabin, surrounded by much colder water, grew chilly. The men received a telephone call from the surface and were interested to learn that a rain squall was in progress up there, far from their dark and timeless world of water and of silence.

Now they plunged past the depths they had attained in early test dives. They were descending into territory never penetrated by man, at depths that no man had ever been able to reach alive. Thirty thousand feet down they noted a sudden absence of plankton as they admired the limpid clarity of the water. With only about a mile to go, they cast off ballast at an accelerated rate, to slow down their descent into the unknown. From now on they were putting their trust in calculations, much as the orbiters of the moon were to do eight years later. These calculations indicated that *Trieste* could indeed withstand the pressures she was encountering at this depth, but neither man nor robot had ever taken her down to prove it.

Down, down, down. . . . What would they land on, or in? Who could be sure how deep the ooze would be, nearly seven miles below the surface of the sea? Down, down, down. . . . In the silence each man could hear the beat of his own heart. And then they landed on a smooth flat bottom at the deepest place in inner space. They were 35,-800 feet below the surface of the Pacific Ocean, with 200,000 tons of pressure *per square inch* outside there on the other side of the thin walls of their vessel's cabin pushing against them! At this historic moment Jacques Piccard forgot that awesome fact. He was filled with excitement for a very different reason. He had spied a fish, a real fish with a backbone and resembling a sole, a fish at least a foot long! Here at the greatest depth of all the world's seas he had found the answer, once and for all, to the question that scientists had pondered and debated. Could fish live in the abyssal depths? They could. They did!

But what had Auguste Piccard been doing while his son Jacques, using the tool forged by the two of them, was preparing for the greatest dive of them all. He had gone back to his quiet study on the banks of Lake Geneva, and he had also gone back to making plans. He was now almost eighty, but his brain was as active as ever. He had a wonderful new idea, one which would merge his two interests, space and oceanography, and he could hardly wait for Jacques, who had made sixty-five previous dives in the *Trieste*, to make his valedictory descent to the floor of the Challenger Deep. Auguste Piccard never doubted that his son would succeed. Then he would ask Jacques to join him in a new undertaking. It was to be a vessel that combined the properties of a submarine and helicopter, to operate at about four thousand feet undersea, gathering marine life from the rich middle depths with robot hands. . . . He would call it a *mesoscaphe* from the Greek *mesos* (middle) *scaphos* (boat).

Jacques too, was enthused with his father's new idea. After his final great descent he and Lieutenant Walsh were flown to Washington on a naval plane to be decorated by President Eisenhower. Then Jacques Piccard came home to Switzerland to join his father. Once again the two men began a familiar process . . . gathering funds as they progressed. The money came easier this time, for they were famous. Work on the mesoscaphe was under way. Then, in June of 1962, in the seventy-eighth year of his life, Auguste Piccard's old heart gave out. For so many years it had been subjected to so many stresses that no one could wonder at his sudden death. . . .

Although grieving, Madame Piccard was deeply aware of her good fortune. Her husband had known rare joy — a combination of personal happiness and ambitions realized. His name would endure forever. One of the world's great pioneers, he had lived to achieve his dreams in two separate fields and in two different directions. His son was

Auguste Piccard's last undertaking was the plan for a mesoscaphe. Jacques continued work after the death of his father and gave the mesoscaphe the only possible appropriate name.

carrying on his work and would add new luster to the name of Piccard. But to her, the greatest miracle of them all was one that she had never dared to hope for. Her husband had not died violently, at some unimaginable height or depth, as she had so often dreaded in the long watches of the night. Instead, his end had come quietly, at home, and in their own bed!

Adelaide Anderson Field

AUTHOR'S NOTE

AUGUSTE PICCARD's inventions have brought into being a veritable stream of others. It has been said that "only interplanetary navigation is likely to raise problems as detailed and complicated." Many many minds will pool their ideas and knowledge to resolve those problems. One mind, that of Auguste Piccard, resolved all the major problems presented by the bathyscaphe. In his stratospheric balloon he climbed ten miles. His bathyscaphe *Trieste* descended nearly seven miles. The sum of the two journeys is under twenty miles. This short course opened up the universe to man. Others, yet unborn, will add their links to the long chain of scientific achievements that lengthens with each succeeding generation.

Jacques Piccard completed the mesoscaphe that he and his father began together. He called it the *Auguste Piccard*, naming it for the man who had never named anything for himself. It was launched on February 27, 1964, for the Swiss Exposition at Lausanne.

In 1968, under the auspices of Grumman Aircraft Company, Jacques Piccard supervised the construction of a second mesoscaphe. Its purpose . . . the 1969 Gulf Stream underwater drift from Florida to Cape Cod . . . to study and mine, over a one-month submerged period, the vast and varied marine life of the rich middle depths.

VENT

WATER BALLAST TANK

PROPELLERS

GASOLINE TANKS

FLOODLAMPS

RELEASE MAGNETS

PELLET BALLAST HOPPER

BALLAST RELEASE MAGNET

ELECTRONIC FLASH

WINDOW

SNORKEL

PRESSURE RELEASE VALVE

OBSERVATION GONDOLA

ENTRANCE TUNNEL

HATCH

PELLET BALLAST HOPPER

BALLAST RELEASE MAGNET

RELEASE MAGNETS

GASOLINE TANKS

GUIDE ROPE

VENT

WATER BALLAST TANK

Official U.S. Navy Photograph

ACKNOWLEDGMENTS

THE AUTHOR wishes to express her grateful thanks to Marianne Denis Piccard, widow of Auguste Piccard, for giving her many pictures and stories of her husband's boyhood, while she was in their home in Lausanne, Switzerland, in the autumn of 1968. Thanks are also extended to Dr. Jacques Piccard for technical clarification of the manuscript, to Hélène Piccard, daughter of Professor Piccard, and to many other librarians here and in Europe, for assistance in research. She is also indebted to Dr. Edward Zarudski of the Woods Hole Oceanographic Laboratory for making available the facilities of its library, and to Dr. Alyn Vine, inventor of the submersible *Alvin* for his explanation to her of the debt that oceanography owes to Auguste Piccard. Last but not least, she thanks her husband Leverett Cummings for his patience, understanding, cooperation and helpful suggestions during the long months required to write this book.

GLOSSARY TERMS

AIR

The invisible, odorless and tasteless mixture of gases which surrounds the earth.

AIR LOCK

An intermediate chamber between the outer air and the inside chamber.

AIR PRESSURE

Force exerted by air against an object at sea level it is 14.7 to the square inch. It decreases in altitudes, increases in depths below sea level.

ABYSSAL

Pertaining to the bottom waters of the sea.

ABYSSAL DEPTHS

Term used for areas of the ocean more than a mile deep, beyond the Continental Slopes.

ATMOSPHERE

The whole mass of air surrounding the earth.

BALLAST

Heavy material used in a balloon or vessel to control its rise or descent, or to improve its stability. Iron pellets were used in Piccard's bathyscaphes.

BAROMETER

An instrument for determining atmospheric pressure and hence for judging probable changes of weather. Also for ascertaining height of an ascent.

BUOYANCY

Ability of an object to float in water or air. *Positive* buoyancy causes an object to float upward against gravity.

Neutral buoyancy will enable it to float at any level. *Negative* buoyancy makes it sink to the bottom.

CAPTIVE BALLOON

One which is tethered by a rope to the ground, so that it can only rise to a given height.

COSMIC RAY

Rays of extremely high frequency and penetrating power produced beyond the earth's atmosphere. They bombard the earth and are in part responsible for the ionization of earth's atmosphere.

CORROSION (marine)

Rusting and wearing away of metals when exposed to sea water.

DENSITY

The weight of cubic unit volume of any matter.

ELECTROMAGNET

A core of iron magnetic material surrounded by a coil of wire through which an electric current is passed to magnetize the core.

ENVELOPE

In a balloon, the bag which contains the gas.

FREE BALLOON

One which is not tethered to the ground, but is free to travel in the wind.

GONDOLA

Underpart of an airship or balloon.

HULL

Body of a ship or submarine, usually built over a reinforcing skeleton.

144

Conveying or acting by water; operated or affected by water.

An inflammable gas, lighter than any other substance.

An electrified particle.

The process of converting into ions.

A material used to prevent loss or transfer of heat, sound or electricity.

That branch of physics dealing with the atmosphere and its phenomena, especially with its variations of heat, moisture, winds.

A colorless gaseous element, tasteless and odorless, constituting 78.03 percent of the atmosphere by volume. A constituent of all living tissues.

Crushing force exerted by sea water on the surface of a submerged body. Usually expressed in pounds per square inch. At sea level it is 14.7. After the first 33 feet of descent, where it doubles, it then increases by 15 pounds per square inch for each additional 15 feet of descent.

Air which is thin, in high altitude.

The upper portion of the atmosphere above 7½ miles (11

kilometers) where clouds and water never form, and where temperature changes very little.

SEDIMENT

The matter which settles to the bottom of the sea.

SONIC

Pertaining to sound.

SALINITY

Degree of saltiness.

SCUBA DIVER

A diver equipped with an air tank enabling him to remain below the surface of the sea while the supply of air lasts. He can penetrate to depths of around 250 feet safely.

THERMAL

Pertaining to heat.

TROPOSPHERE

All that portion of the atmosphere below the stratosphere.

ZENITH

The upper pole of horizon. Summit. Peak.

PROPER NAMES

ARISTOTLE

Greek philosopher (384–322 B.C.).

BEEBE, WILLIAM

Inventor of bathysphere, in which, with his engineer Otis Barton, he made the first deep human penetration of the ocean depths. His vessel was tethered to a surface ship.

BENNETT, JAMES GORDON

Publisher of New York *Herald*, donor of Gordon Cup for transoceanic balloon races prior to World War II.

COPERNICUS

Polish astronomer (1473–1543). He elaborated an entirely new system of astronomy by the adoption of which man's outlook on the universe was fundamentally changed. First man to use hydrogen in a balloon.

CHARLES, JACQUES

Famous early balloonist.

CHALLENGER DEEP

Lowest known area of all the world's seas, 35,800 feet below the surface, in the Pacific Ocean near Guam.

COUSTEAU, JACQUES

Famous French scuba diver.

DE ROZIER, PILATRE

King's historian to Louis XVI. First man to go up in a balloon. His first ascension was in a tethered balloon. He also made the first manned free flight. He died in a balloon explosion, where hydrogen gas was used.

GALILEO

Italian astronomer and experimental philosopher (1564–1642). A mathematician, he succeeded in producing a telescope with a magnification of 32, and manufactured hundreds of them with his own hands. He showed that the Milky Way is a collection of stars.

HALLEY EDMUND

English astronomer (1656–1742). Discovered a new comet which comes within earth's range only once every seventy-five years. It bears his name.

LOUIS XVI

King of France who ascended throne at age of twenty (1774). Married Marie Antoinette.

MONTGOLFIER, ÉTIENNE and JACQUES

Two French schoolboys who "invented" the balloon by accident, then went on to perfect this simplest form of aircraft.

NOBEL, ALFRED

Swedish chemist and engineer (1833–1896). Inventor of dynamite which he patented in 1862. Donor of the Nobel prizes (for physics, chemistry, medicine, literature and peace.) Only Madame Curie, honored in both physics and mathematics, has been awarded more than one Nobel prize.

PLATO

Greek philosopher and poet (*c*. 427 B.C.–*c*. 347 B.C.).

PICCARD, MARIANNE DENIS

Wife of Auguste Piccard, mother of Jacques Piccard.

THOMSON, CHARLES WYVILLE

Eighteenth century professor, who, on an epochal 3½-year-voyage around the world, discovered many new marine species and was knighted for his contributions to the new science of oceanography.

WALSH, DONALD

Lieutenant, United States Navy, who accompanied

Jacques Piccard on his record-setting descent to the bottom of the Marianas Trench in the Challenger Deep.

WRIGHT, ORVILLE and WILBUR

Two bicycle manufacturers from Dayton, Ohio, who made first airplane flight at Kitty Hawk, North Carolina, in December 1903.

BIBLIOGRAPHY

BOOKS

Cook, J. Gordon, *Exploring Under the Sea*. New York: Abelard-Schuman, 1964.

De Latil, Pierre, and Revoire, Jean, *Man and the Underwater World*. New York: G. P. Putnam & Sons.

Dugan, James, *Men Under the Sea*. New York: Harper Bros., 1956.

Honour, Alan, *Ten Miles High, Two Miles Deep*. New York: Whittlesey House, 1957.

Piccard, Auguste, *Earth, Sky and Sea*. New York: Oxford University Press, 1956.

Piccard, Jacques, and Dietz, Robert, *Seven Miles Down*. New York: G. P. Putnam and Sons, 1960.

Wagner, Frederick, *Famous Underwater Adventurers*. New York: Dodd, Mead, 1962.

PERIODICALS

American Mercury, February 1954.

Collier's Year Book, 1954.

Life, October 12, 1953.

The Literary Digest, June 13, 1931.

National Geographic Magazine, July 1954, May 1958.

Newsweek, April 12, 1954, February 5, 1961, January 25, 1960, August 11, 1958.

Science Digest, May 1955.

Scientific American, April, 1958.

Skin Diver Magazine, August, 1961.

Time, June 6, 1962, July 8, 1946, August 18, 1947, October 12, 1953.

Also the London *Times* and many French- and German-language scientific journals were consulted.